THE ULTIMATE LLC BEGINNER'S GUIDE

YOUR ALL-IN-ONE SOURCE TO FORM, MANAGE, AND GROW A SUCCESSFUL LIMITED LIABILITY COMPANY - START A BUSINESS EVEN WITH ZERO EXPERIENCE

BRENT GOLDWYN

Copyright © 2025 Brent Goldwyn

All rights reserved. No part of this book may be reproduced, stored in a retrieval system, or transmitted in any form or by any means—electronic, mechanical, photocopying, recording, or otherwise—without the prior written permission of the author or publisher, except as permitted under U.S. copyright law.

Disclaimer

This book is provided for informational and educational purposes only. While every effort has been made to present accurate, up-to-date, and reliable information, it should not be considered legal, financial, or tax advice. The author and publisher are not attorneys, accountants, or financial advisors. Laws and regulations vary by jurisdiction and are subject to change. Readers should consult a licensed professional before making any business, financial, or legal decisions.

The author and publisher make no warranties, express or implied, regarding the accuracy, reliability, or completeness of this information. They assume no responsibility for errors, omissions, or outcomes related to the use of this book. By reading this publication, the reader agrees that the author and publisher shall not be held liable for any direct, indirect, incidental, consequential, or punitive damages resulting from the use of this material.

Trademarks

All trademarks, service marks, product names, or named features mentioned in this book are the property of their respective owners. The use of such names does not imply endorsement, sponsorship, or affiliation with this publication.

ISBN 13: 978-1-967516-01-8 (Paperback edition)

Published by: LLC Champion, an imprint of Jackfruit Publishing

Printed in the United States of America

For more information, visit: **www.llcchampion.com**

MAXIMIZE YOUR SUCCESS AND GET THE MOST OUT OF THIS BOOK

Scan the QR Code Below to Download Your Bonuses!

Setting up your LLC just got easier. Scan the QR code below to access these **6 powerful free resources** that will save you **time, money, and stress.**

📌 **BONUS 1: LLC Formation Checklist**

⚠️ **BONUS 2: 5 Mistakes Beginners Make When Starting an LLC**

🌍 **BONUS 3: Best Websites for Starting Your LLC**

🏛️ **BONUS 4: The Ultimate State-By-State Formation Guide**

📜 **BONUS 5: LLC Operating Agreement Template**

📊 **BONUS 6: Business Plan Template**

Claim Your Exclusive Bonuses Now – Just Scan Below!

Or visit the following link to access them now:
https://unlockbonuses.llcchampion.com/llc

CONTENTS

Introduction   ix

1. UNDERSTANDING THE BASICS   1
   What Is an LLC?   1
   Common Myths and Misconceptions About LLCs   7
   LLC vs. Other Business Structures: Making the Right Choice   8

2. PRE-FORMATION CONSIDERATIONS   13
   Choosing Your LLC Name: Legal Requirements and Creative Tips   13
   Determining Your LLC's Business Purpose and Goals   16
   Selecting Your LLC's Registered Agent   20
   Understanding the Importance of a Business Plan for Your LLC   22
   Action Steps   26

3. ESTABLISHING YOUR LLC: THE FORMATION PROCESS   31
   Filing Articles of Organization   31
   Getting Your EIN   34
   Smooth Operator: Creating an Operating Agreement   35
   Initial Member Contributions and Capital Accounts   38
   Action Steps for Forming Your LLC   41

4. LEGAL AND COMPLIANCE ESSENTIALS ... 43
   Annual Reports and Ongoing Compliance Obligations ... 43
   Understanding State-Specific LLC Requirements ... 47
   Understanding and Managing Business Licenses and Permits ... 49
   Common Legal Pitfalls and How to Avoid Them ... 51
   Utilizing Professional Services: When to Consult an Attorney or Accountant ... 52

5. TAX STRATEGIES AND BENEFITS ... 55
   Taxation Basics for LLCs: What You Need to Know ... 55
   Understanding Pass-Through Taxation and Its Benefits ... 57
   Electing S-Corp Status: Pros, Cons, and Process ... 59
   Advanced Tax Strategies for LLC Owners ... 62

   Success: A Shift In Perspective ... 67

6. FINANCIAL MANAGEMENT ... 69
   Setting Up Your LLC's Bank Accounts and Financial Systems ... 69
   Handling Business Debt and Credit ... 72
   Budgeting and Financial Planning for Your LLC ... 74
   Understanding and Preparing Financial Statements ... 76
   Preparing for Tax Season: Record-Keeping and Deductions ... 78

7. GROWTH AND SCALING STRATEGIES 81
   Marketing Your LLC: Strategies for Growth . . 81
   Securing Financing: Loans, Investors, and
   Grants 85
   Scaling Operations: Hiring, Outsourcing,
   and Automation 88
   Expanding Your LLC: New Markets and
   Products 91

8. RISK MANAGEMENT AND LIABILITY
   PROTECTION 97
   Types of Risk 98
   Risk Assessment 100
   Risk Management Techniques 101
   Types of Insurance 102
   Applying Risk Management to Business
   Growth 104
   Action Steps 107

9. OPERATIONAL EXCELLENCE 109
   Effective Time Management for LLC
   Owners 110
   Building a Strong Team: Recruiting and
   Retaining Talent 112
   Utilizing Technology to Streamline
   Operations 114
   Customer Relationship Management: Best
   Practices 116

10. EXIT STRATEGIES AND SUCCESSION
    PLANNING 119
    Planning Your Exit Strategy: Options and
    Considerations 119
    Valuing Your LLC: Methods and Factors . . 123

Selling Your LLC: Process and Tips	125
Succession Planning: Passing Your LLC to the Next Generation	128
Dissolving Your LLC: Legal and Financial Steps	130

11. **INTERNATIONAL ENTREPRENEURS** — 133

Forming an LLC as a Non-U.S. Resident: Key Steps	133
Working Through US Business Regulations as an International Entrepreneur	137
Leveraging US Market Opportunities: Tips for Success	140
Your Review, Their Inspiration	143
Conclusion	145
References	147

INTRODUCTION

"Why did you choose to get an LLC?" I asked my friend Dean. "For my traveling nurse job, then my IV business," he replied. Dean had started as a roving nurse but decided to supplement his income with a side gig that provides mobile IV therapy and wellness services to clients at their homes or offices.

Still, the question remained: "But why specifically an LLC?"

"Well ... I know they're good for tax reasons. Like, I can deduct flights, gas, food ... the flexibility is great for keeping my expenses down. But honestly, I don't know much beyond that. Just that everyone says LLCs are the way to go."

It wasn't just Dean's story that stuck with me—it was a reflection of a common scenario many aspiring business owners face. They've heard LLCs are important, maybe even necessary, but they don't really know why or how to leverage their full potential. And in many cases, they don't even know where to begin. If that sounds familiar, this book is for you.

Welcome to *The Ultimate LLC Beginner's Guide.* Whether you're a side hustler, small business owner, or aspiring entrepreneur, the goal of this book is to demystify the process of starting and running an LLC. With simple instructions, actionable insights, and easy-to-follow examples, you'll confidently learn how to form, manage, and scale your LLC. Don't feel like you have to already know what you're doing or even be familiar with the technical jargon; the goal here is to be accessible for complete beginners. Whether you already own a business, want to form an LLC, or are brand new to the topic, this book can meet your needs.

Legal requirements, tax considerations, and risk management can be intimidating, especially if it all initially sounds so foreign. But there are ways to simplify the process and provide the knowledge and tools you need to succeed—and that's why I'm here. When we're done, hopefully, you'll think of this text as a comprehensive resource that has equipped you with everything you need to build a successful LLC.

Forming and managing an LLC is more doable than it might seem now. Even with no prior experience, you can still achieve your business goals. So, let's work together to turn your dreams into reality and build a successful LLC that stands the test of time.

1

UNDERSTANDING THE BASICS

Starting a business is one of the most rewarding yet challenging moves an entrepreneur can make. As an example, let's talk about Hannah, a talented baker whose evolution from crafting beautiful desserts to managing legal and financial business complexities highlights common challenges for new business owners. Hannah was advised to form an LLC but had no idea what that entailed. Where she went from there is an instructive example for you to follow.

But let's start with the basics first, beginning with the simplest question there is: What even is an LLC, anyway?

WHAT IS AN LLC?

A limited liability company, or LLC, is a business structure that combines the operational flexibility and tax benefits of a partnership or sole proprietorship with the **limited liability protection** of a corporation. This hybrid nature appeals to many entrepreneurs because it shields personal assets from business debts and lawsuits while offering tax efficiency. The idea is that it's designed to be the best of both worlds for small business owners and entrepreneurs.

The term "limited liability" means that as an owner (also known as a member), your personal assets are protected from the financial risks associated with your work. If your business encounters financial trouble or is sued, creditors can't go after your personal property like your home, car, or personal savings. This protection is particularly valuable for small business owners who want to safeguard their personal wealth, where an LLC effectively acts as a shield that separates one's personal life from their professional one (Tyler 2024).

In Hannah's case, she decided to form an LLC for her bakery, Sweet Stuff, because of the liability protection it offers. When a batch of cupcakes at Hannah's bakery causes a food-borne illness, the customers sue her business for damages. Thanks to the LLC structure, only the bakery's assets—not Hannah's personal property—are at risk. Because of the LLC structure, Hannah can sell equipment, liquidate business assets, or use the emergency fund to pay the settlement, but the other party (in this case, the customers) can't legally seize her personal assets or savings. Hannah and her customers ultimately agree to settle for $100,000—none of which impacts what Hannah had saved for herself separate from the business. This level of security can provide you with peace of mind, allowing you to focus on growing your business without the constant worry of risking personal financial ruin.

One quick note before we move on: This fiscal protection is not always guaranteed. A court can hold you personally liable through what is known as "piercing the corporate veil." Chapter 8, *Risk Management and Liability Protection*, will cover the methods to prevent this from happening, though, so stay tuned.

Corporations actually also have a liability shield—but unlike a corporation, an LLC avoids double taxation. Instead, it benefits from what's known as **pass-through taxation**, meaning the business's income is reported directly on the owners' personal tax returns. Instead of paying corporate income tax on the annual profit and then dividend tax on the dividends paid out to its shareholders, LLC members only pay tax on this income when they file their taxes for that year—hence, single taxation rather than double (Thomson Reuters 2024).

Let's assume Hannah has a business partner named Richard. After paying salaries and other expenses, Sweet Stuff LLC makes an annual profit of $90,000 at the end of the year. Because it's not a corporation, it doesn't pay a corporate tax; instead, the tax "passes through" to its members, Hannah and Richard. The two of them split the profit and ultimately report the $45,000 as income on their respective tax returns. This setup simplifies tax filing and can result in significant tax savings, as each of them only pays taxes on their individual income rather than the business itself.

A Brief History of LLCs

The birth of the LLC was nothing short of a revolution in American business law. First introduced in Wyoming in 1977, LLCs completely changed how business owners structured their companies. By combining the liability protection traditionally offered by corporations with the tax simplicity of partnerships, LLCs redefined how businesses were formed. LLCs have since become a popular choice for US businesses, particularly small businesses and startups. Following Wyoming's lead, all fifty states and the District of Columbia had enacted LLC statutes by 1996. Today, LLCs are an extremely popular business entity in the US, a testament to their appeal and effectiveness across different industries (Hamill 1998).

Benefits of Choosing an LLC

In addition to limited liability protection and pass-through taxation—two big advantages that shield personal assets and simplify tax reporting—LLCs offer a range of other significant benefits that make them an attractive option for business owners.

Tax Flexibility and Benefits

One of the most appealing features of an LLC is its tax flexibility. While avoiding double taxation, LLCs also allow business owners to deduct legitimate business expenses such as rent, utilities, salaries, and office supplies. These deductions can significantly reduce taxable income, leading to substantial tax savings. LLC owners can also make tax-deductible contributions to retirement plans and health insurance premiums, providing additional financial security and further reducing overall tax burdens (Chafin 2024).

Another unique feature of LLCs is their ability to elect a different tax status. Owners can choose to have their LLC taxed as a sole proprietorship, partnership, S-Corporation (S-Corp), or C-Corporation (C-Corp), depending on their business goals and tax optimization strategy. For example, electing to be taxed as an S-Corp can help reduce self-employment taxes for owners who pay themselves a salary, offering a strategic advantage for tax savings. The money you save could then be used to reinvest into the business, thus making you more money in the long run (Nelson 2024). We'll get into this more in Chapter 5.

Credibility and Long-Term Stability

There's a credibility bonus to an LLC, too. Forming an LLC establishes it as an independent legal entity, adding a layer of professionalism and showing clients, lenders, and suppliers that you've taken formal steps to operate legally. Having contacts recognize your business as a legitimate operation can lead to more trust and easier access to partnerships or vendor agreements.

Another significant benefit of registering as an LLC is the ease of establishing business credit in the company's name. With an LLC, you can build credit tied to your Employer Identification Number (EIN) rather than your social security number. This means you can open business bank accounts, apply for loans, and build a credit history unique to your business, creating a foundation of financial reliability for future growth (Ho. Johnson 2024).

Additionally, LLCs provide structural longevity. Unlike partnerships, an LLC remains intact even if a member leaves, giving it a sturdy level of stability through ownership transfers or sales. Creditors also cannot force dissolution if financial troubles arise, giving your business a better chance to recover and continue even after overcoming financial hurdles. LLCs, far more than some other types of business arrangements, are designed to be difficult to get rid of (Vethan Law Firm, P.C. 2017).

· · ·

Adaptable Ownership and Management

One of the defining features of LLCs is their adaptability, offering an ownership and management structure that can cater to various business sizes and types. LLC members can be individuals, corporations, or foreign entities without limits on the number of members. An LLC can actually even be owned by another LLC, which seems like a strange practice but is actually quite common (Willis 2023). This adaptability makes LLCs a versatile choice for both small businesses and larger enterprises, enabling you to tailor the structure to your specific business needs.

LLCs offer business owners a choice in management style. In a **member-managed** LLC, all members are involved in daily operations and decision-making, a popular choice for small businesses where owners want to be hands-on. On the other hand, a **manager-managed** LLC allows members to appoint managers to handle daily operations—ideal for owners who prefer a more passive role. Depending on the chosen management structure, business owners can tailor their LLCs to their specific needs, making them an excellent option for businesses of all sizes (Prakash 2020).

Operational Flexibility and Profit Distribution

Unlike corporations, which often require a board of directors, regular meetings, and extensive record-keeping, LLC owners are not bound by rigid corporate formalities, giving them greater freedom to manage their business as they see fit. This reduction in paperwork allows business owners to focus on growing their businesses rather than getting bogged down with compliance tasks or spinning plates to keep tons of shareholders happy at once.

Moreover, LLCs offer flexibility in how profits are distributed. Members can decide how profits are divided, which doesn't necessarily have to follow the strict ownership percentages required in corporations. This allows for more personalized and creative financial arrangements among members, which can be particularly beneficial for businesses with varying levels of owner involvement (Woodside 2024).

For small businesses and startups in particular, the combination of limited liability protection and significant tax benefits creates a solid foundation for growth. Take, for example, a freelance graphic designer who wants to formalize their business while protecting personal assets. An LLC would offer them the perfect blend of simplicity and professionalism. Consultants who provide professional advice can also benefit from an LLC's liability protection so that their advice can never be weaponized against them if it goes wrong. Family-owned businesses, meanwhile, often find LLCs advantageous because they offer a straightforward way to manage and distribute profits among family members.

COMMON MYTHS AND MISCONCEPTIONS ABOUT LLCS

A common misconception is that LLCs are only suitable for small businesses. This is far from accurate. LLCs can benefit businesses of all sizes and industries. Many large companies, including well-known names like Google, PepsiCo, and Exxon Mobil, have LLC subsidiaries or are structured as LLCs (Upcounsel 2020). The flexibility, liability protection, and tax benefits make LLCs a practical choice, regardless of a company's size.

Another widespread myth is that forming an LLC is a complicated and costly process. While it does involve some paperwork, the steps are surprisingly straightforward and manageable. Misunderstandings about LLC taxation are also common. For example, some believe that forming an LLC will automatically reduce taxes, but it actually depends on which tax structure you choose. By default, single-member LLCs are taxed as sole proprietorships, and multi-member LLCs are taxed as partnerships. However, LLCs can opt to be taxed as an S-Corp or C-Corp.

Another myth is that LLCs don't offer significant legal protection. In reality, LLCs provide legal protection; however, this protection isn't absolute. If members personally guarantee loans or engage in fraudulent activity, their personal assets could be at risk. The best way to avoid this is pretty clearly to stick to proper business practices, such as keeping personal and business finances separate and adhering to the operating agreement. Basically, don't commit fraud.

LLC VS. OTHER BUSINESS STRUCTURES: MAKING THE RIGHT CHOICE

Choosing the proper business structure is fundamental for any entrepreneur, as each structure has unique features and implications for liability, taxation, and operational flexibility. Let's examine how an LLC compares to other popular structures—sole proprietorships, partnerships, and corporations—to help you make an informed decision.

Sole Proprietorship

A sole proprietorship is the simplest business structure and is ideal for solo entrepreneurs who want complete control over their operations and profits. Setting up a sole proprietorship is easy, with minimal paperwork: You only need to obtain any required permits or licenses for your business. You're not even required to file formation documents like LLCs or corporations. This simplicity, though, comes with a major trade-off: unlimited personal liability. Since the business and owner are legally the same entity, you are personally liable for any debts or lawsuits that arise, putting personal assets such as your home or savings at risk if the business fails or faces legal issues.

A sole proprietorship may be convenient for entrepreneurs with low-risk ventures or who are just starting out. But, if you anticipate taking on significant debt or hiring employees soon, you may benefit from exploring other structures with better liability protections (Huston 2023).

Partnership

In a partnership, two or more individuals share ownership, responsibilities, and profits. While partnerships are relatively easy to form and do not require state registration, partners often draft a partnership agreement to clarify profit-sharing, decision-making, and ownership stakes. This agreement, which should also outline procedures for adding or removing partners and resolving conflicts, can help prevent misunderstandings and keep the business running smoothly (Huston 2021).

Like sole proprietorships, general partnerships expose partners to unlimited liability, meaning each partner is personally liable for business debts and obligations. Limited partnerships offer some protection to limited partners, who are only liable for the amount they invested, but general partners still face full liability. Partnerships are best suited to small groups who want to share responsibilities and resources without the complexities inherent in more formal structures. However, if liability is a concern in general, an LLC might offer members more protection and flexibility than a partnership does.

Corporation

Corporations are unique because they exist as separate legal entities, providing the strongest liability protection for their owners. Shareholders in a corporation are typically not personally liable for business debts, meaning their risk is limited to the amount they have invested in the company. This structure also makes it easier to raise capital by issuing shares, which can be sold to investors (Edwards 2024).

However, corporations come with significant drawbacks. The most notable is double taxation: Corporate profits are taxed at the company level, and any dividends paid to shareholders are taxed again on their personal income returns. Additionally, corporations require more stringent record-keeping and compliance, including holding regular shareholder meetings, filing annual reports, and maintaining detailed records to meet state regulations. These formalities make corporations more complex and costly to operate, which can be prohibitive for startups and small businesses. As a company grows and seeks outside investment, it may see some benefit to transitioning to a corporate structure.

Example: Pros and Cons of Each Business Structure

BUSINESS STRUCTURE	PROS	CONS
Sole Proprietorship	Easy setup, minimal paperwork, full control by owner	Unlimited personal liability, harder to raise capital, less professional image
Partnership	Simple to establish, shared financial commitment, pass-through taxation	Unlimited liability for general partners, potential conflicts among partners
LLC	Limited liability protection, pass-through taxation, flexible management structure	Formation fees, self-employment taxes, more paperwork than sole proprietorships
C-Corporation	Limited Liability, ability to raise capital, potential tax benefits	Double taxation, complex regulations, extensive record-keeping
S-Corporation	Limited liability, pass-through taxation, potential self-employment tax savings	Strict eligibility, limited shareholders, more regulatory oversight than LLCs

Ultimately, it's your choice to form whichever type of business entity suits your entrepreneurial aspirations. Each can help you establish a foundation that supports long-term growth, depending on the situation—although, as we've talked about, LLCs have some pretty significant benefits. Ultimately, understanding LLCs and how they compare to other structures prepares you to make an informed decision.

2

PRE-FORMATION CONSIDERATIONS

When Carla decided to start her high-quality cleaning business, she was excited but quickly realized that she needed to choose the right name for her company before she could form an LLC. She learned what every new LLC owner learns: A business name is more than just a label—it's a first impression. She also learned that it has to not only reflect her brand's identity but also meet legal requirements. Obviously, you cannot ignore these.

CHOOSING YOUR LLC NAME: LEGAL REQUIREMENTS AND CREATIVE TIPS

Naming your LLC is one of the first steps to forming your business, but more goes into it than just coming up with something catchy. Each state has specific rules for LLC names, and understanding these rules is essential. Your LLC name must include an indication that it's a limited liability company, like "LLC," "L.L.C.," "Limited Liability Co.," or "Limited." Anyone interacting with your business needs to know it's an LLC and understand its legal structure as well as the liability protections it offers (d'Viola 2022).

Additionally, the name must be unique and distinguishable from other businesses operating within the state to prevent confusion and maintain brand clarity. This is why you're not allowed to call your business "Google"—which operates everywhere—but you could call a pizza place "Mel's Pizza" if there are no other Mel's Pizzas in your state. There are other rules, too: Certain words, like "bank," "insurance," or any terms related to government agencies (e.g., "FBI," "Treasury"), are restricted. These are either entirely prohibited or require special permissions to use.

Creativity also plays a significant role in naming your LLC, with your guiding stars being "simple" and "catchy." Your business name should thus be memorable, easy to spell, and reflective of your brand's identity. Start with brainstorming sessions, jotting down all the words and phrases that come to mind when you think about your business. If you're really stuck, there are name-generation tools available online that can provide a plethora of suggestions based on the keywords you input. Think about your brand's market positioning—how you want to be perceived by your target audience. A good name can convey your business's values, mission, or unique selling proposition. For instance, Carla's cleaning business could benefit from a name like "Carla Can Clean LLC," which immediately conveys the nature of her high-quality cleaning services while leaning on the catchy, memorable nature of alliteration.

Conducting Availability Checks

Before settling on a name, conduct a thorough availability check to make sure your chosen name isn't already in use. Your state's business registry is a great place to start; most states offer online databases where you can quickly check the availability of your desired name just by searching for it. It's also wise to check for any potential trademark conflicts with the US Patent and Trademark Office (USPTO). A federal trademark provides national protection for your business name, something state registration alone doesn't guarantee. Do this first thing because conducting a trademark search early in the process can save you from costly rebranding efforts down the line. You can also perform an initial screening search yourself or hire a trademark attorney for a more comprehensive search (Beaulieu 2024).

"Domain"-ating the Competition

It's also a good idea to secure a matching domain name for your LLC to establish a consistent online presence since you're likely going to need some sort of online presence. Once you have a shortlist of potential names for the business itself, check if the corresponding domain names are available. Use domain registration websites to find and secure your desired domain promptly; some popular ones include GoDaddy, Hostinger, Namecheap, and Squarespace (formerly Google Domains). Securing your preferred domain name early on is an excellent way to strengthen your brand and avoid future issues. If Carla chooses "Carla Can Clean LLC" as her business name, securing the domain "carlacanclean.com" would help establish her brand across platforms and make it easy for customers to find her online.

DETERMINING YOUR LLC'S BUSINESS PURPOSE AND GOALS

Establishing a clear business purpose helps define your LLC's direction and communicates its mission. A well-crafted purpose statement should be specific enough to guide daily operations but broad enough to support future growth. Something like **"Our mission is to deliver reliable, high-quality cleaning services to promote healthier living environments"** is concise, memorable, and conveys your value.

Setting SMART Goals

One good idea to make your goals effective is to utilize the SMART framework. Conceived by businessman George Doran in 1981, SMART is designed to help businesses streamline their goal-setting efficiency (Abbott 2024). The various parts of the acronym and what they stand for:

- **Specific**: Define what you want to achieve.
- **Measurable**: Include criteria to track progress.
- **Achievable**: Set realistic objectives within reach.
- **Relevant**: Align goals with your overall mission.
- **Time-bound**: Establish a clear deadline.

Short-term Goals

Short-term goals are the immediate steps you'll take within the next year to build momentum. Rather than the big picture, these are intended to be actionable benchmarks you set for yourself to measure your progress. Examples might include:

- Launch your website within three months.
- Gain your first fifty clients within six months through local promotions.

Long-term Goals

Long-term goals outline where you want the business to go in the next three to five years. This is the bigger picture, where you figure out the business's overall direction. These can include:

- Expand to a new city by year three.
- Reach annual revenue milestones to support service innovation.

Using a SWOT Analysis for Strategic Planning

A SWOT analysis helps you identify your business's Strengths, Weaknesses, Opportunities, and Threats. SWOT is built to be impartial and tell hard truths about the state of your business so you can address issues that might get in the way of your future potential. For a high-quality cleaning business, this tool can clarify your unique advantages, potential challenges, and areas to focus on for growth (Kenton 2024a).

STRENGTHS	WEAKNESSES
Commitment to high cleaning standards	Higher costs associated with premium services
Highly trained, professional staff	Limited brand recognition in new markets
Use of quality cleaning products	Smaller customer base compared to competitors
OPPORTUNITIES	**THREATS**
Growing demand for premium cleaning	Established competitors in the area
Potential to expand to luxury clients	Fluctuations in market demand
Ability to capitalize on referrals	Rising costs of quality cleaning supplies

Using SWOT for Strategic Advantage

Once you've completed your SWOT analysis, you can turn insights into actionable strategies. For example:

- **Leverage Strengths**: Use "commitment to high standards" as a key marketing message in advertising to attract clients seeking superior service.
- **Address Weaknesses**: Consider brand-building campaigns to increase recognition, especially in new markets.
- **Capitalize on Opportunities**: Develop referral programs to encourage satisfied clients to refer others, building your client base efficiently.
- **Prepare for Threats**: Monitor competitor

pricing and customer trends to stay competitive in fluctuating market conditions.

Aligning Your Business and Personal Goals

Aligning your business goals with your personal goals keeps your LLC thriving. This part is entirely a thought exercise on your end, but that doesn't make it any less important. Think about what you want to achieve personally through your business: Is it financial independence, more time with family, or the satisfaction of contributing to a cause you care about? Whatever you want out of your LLC, your goal here is to get yourself in the right headspace to pursue it.

Integrating Work-Life Balance

No matter how much of a grindset go-getter you think you are, you're not going to be able to work all the time. Balancing your work-life integration is always going to be important. Instead of just working constantly and risking burnout, set boundaries to guarantee your business doesn't consume all of your time and energy. If one of your goals is to spend more time with family, plan your business schedule to allow for dedicated family time.

This balance doesn't just come down to giving yourself time to recharge, though; you also want to make sure what you're doing is personally fulfilling as well as professionally satisfying. What form this takes is entirely up to you; if your personal fulfillment comes from making a positive impact, align your business activities to support sustainability or community initiatives. This keeps you motivated and makes your pursuit of starting a business rewarding on multiple levels.

In setting your LLC's business purpose and goals, you're laying the groundwork for both immediate solutions and long-term future growth. Establishing this kind of clarity will ultimately help guide your decisions, attract customers, and keep you focused on what truly matters. Whether you aim to dominate your local market, expand nationally, or make a significant social impact, defining your purpose and setting strategic goals puts you on the path to get there.

SELECTING YOUR LLC'S REGISTERED AGENT

A registered agent is an individual or service that acts as your LLC's official contact for receiving legal and compliance documents. This isn't a step to be glossed over or taken lightly; selecting a reliable registered agent is essential to make sure your business receives important communications promptly and remains compliant with state requirements (Wong 2024b).

Individual vs. Professional Services

When choosing a registered agent, you have two primary options: appointing an individual (this can theoretically be yourself) or hiring a professional registered agent service. Here's a quick comparison to help you decide.

INDIVIDUAL REGISTERED AGENT	PROFESSIONAL REGISTERED AGENT
PROS	PROS
Lower or no cost	Reliable coverage and support during business hours
Can be someone familiar with the business	Specialized expertise in handling legal documents
Directly receives important documents	Helps maintain privacy of personal address
CONS	CONS
Must be available during business hours	Service fees apply (typically $100-$300 per year)
May risk missed documents if unavailable	Adds an extra vendor to manage
Uses personal address for public records	

Serving as your own registered agent comes with some organizational requirements that can make it more of a burden. If Carla chooses to serve as her own registered agent for Carla Can Clean, for example, she will need to be consistently available during business hours to receive documents. Alternatively, appointing someone else or hiring a professional service makes sure someone is always available to receive and forward important notices to her, even if she's unavailable at the time.

Steps to Change Your Registered Agent: Carla's Process

Sometimes, for whatever reason, your registered agent needs to be changed after you've already established one. If you need to make a switch, follow these steps, as illustrated by Carla's experience:

1. **Complete Change of Agent Form**: Carla filled out her state's required "Change of Registered Agent" form, available on the state's business filing website.
2. **Notify Current Agent**: Carla notified her current agent of the switch to ensure a smooth transition.
3. **Submit Form and Pay Fee**: She submitted the form and paid a small fee to the state office.
4. **Confirm New Agent's Information**: Finally, Carla double-checked that her new agent's information was correctly updated in all necessary records.

You don't want to just pick any random person; you need to know your registered agent is someone you can trust. Selecting a registered agent carefully helps safeguard your business against potential legal problems, so the reliability and trustworthiness of your registered agent is extremely important. Whether you select an individual or professional service, this decision sets a solid foundation for your LLC's compliance and lets you focus on what really matters to you: growing your business.

UNDERSTANDING THE IMPORTANCE OF A BUSINESS PLAN FOR YOUR LLC

A business plan may seem like an unnecessary document when you already have what you want to do with the business in your head, but it's more important than you might think. Creating a well-structured business plan sets a clear roadmap for success when starting an LLC. It ultimately lays out your vision, aligns your business goals, and serves as a valuable tool when seeking financing or partnerships. By articulating your purpose, target market, and financial projections, a strong business plan becomes your reference point for growth and decision-making if you're ever in doubt (Rich and Gumpert 1985).

10 Key Components of a Business Plan

The ten components of a business plan include:

1. **Executive Summary:** A concise overview of your business, highlighting the mission, goals, and important points of the plan. It should capture attention and make a strong first impression.
2. **Company Description:** Provides detailed information about your business, including its structure, ownership, history, and what makes it unique in the market.
3. **Market Analysis:** Analyzes the industry, market size, trends, and target customers. It also includes competitor analysis to understand where your business fits and how it can stand out amid its peers.
4. **Organization and Management**: Outlines your business's organizational structure, ownership, and management team. Describe the qualifications and roles of your main team members.
5. **Products or Services**: Provides a detailed description of the products or services your business offers. Highlight the benefits and your unique selling points that meet customer needs.
6. **Marketing and Sales Strategy**: Explains how you plan to attract and retain customers. This

should cover pricing, distribution channels, and promotional strategies to drive sales.
7. **Financial Projections**: Includes financial forecasts such as income statements, cash flow projections, and balance sheets. This helps demonstrate your business's profitability and financial health.
8. **Funding Request**: If you're seeking funding, specify the amount needed, how it will be used, and the expected return for investors or lenders.
9. **Risk Analysis**: Identifies potential risks to the business, such as market shifts, operational challenges, and financial uncertainties. Provide strategies for mitigating these risks, helping you create a resilience plan.
10. **Appendix**: Contains additional miscellaneous documents that support your business plan, such as resumes, product photos, permits, or legal agreements.

Benefits of a Business Plan

Having a business plan offers numerous benefits. It's instrumental in securing financing, as lenders and investors often require a detailed plan to understand the potential risks and rewards of getting involved. A business plan also serves as a strategic tool for you, though, clarifying your business direction and helping you set benchmarks and measure your progress, keeping you focused on your goals and providing a reference point for decision-making. Moreover, a business plan can help you identify potential challenges and opportunities you might contend with, allowing you to adapt and pivot as needed.

Writing an effective business plan involves using clear and concise language. Avoid jargon and overly complex sentences; be direct and to the point. Including data and market research is essential, so use credible sources to support your claims and provide a solid foundation for your projections and strategies. Regularly updating your business plan is also important because as your business grows and changes, your plan should reflect that. Review and revise it periodically to keep it relevant and accurate.

Instead of building each section of your plan from scratch, it might be a good idea to use a structured template. This approach covers all the main components without getting you bogged down in details. Download a business plan template to help you outline your business strategy quickly and effectively.

> BONUS: Download our customizable business plan template to guide you step-by-step through building a plan that suits your LLC's unique needs.

Once your business plan has been written, you might want to have it checked by someone else. A second set of eyes can spot things you might've missed, whether that's a friend or an actual professional proofreader. You can also read it out loud to catch typos or unclear language; sometimes it helps to hear it spoken in order to spot issues.

Understanding the importance of a business plan and dedicating time to develop it can significantly impact your LLC's success for the better. By outlining your business vision, strategies, and financial forecasts, you establish a structured and focused approach to building your company.

ACTION STEPS

1. Conduct a State Business Registry Search.
   a. **Access the state business registry**: Start by visiting your Secretary of State's website or the relevant business registry for your state. Each state has an online tool to check name availability. A comprehensive state-by-state listing can also be found in a resource I created called *The Ultimate State-By-State LLC Formation Guide* in the BONUS materials.
   b. **Search for your desired business name**: Enter the name you'd like to use and see if it's available. If the name is already taken, you're going to need to modify it or try entirely different options.
   c. **Example**: Carla wants to register "Carla Can Clean LLC." She goes to her state's business registry, enters the name in the search field, and checks if it appears in the results. "Carla Can Clean LLC" isn't registered, so she's good to proceed with her next steps.
2. Perform a Trademark Search.
   a. **Visit the USPTO Trademark Database**: Go to the U.S. Patent and Trademark Office website and use the Trademark Electronic Search System (TESS). Go to: https://www.uspto.gov/trademarks/search
   b. **Search for potential conflicts**: Just like with the state search, enter the desired name in

the search bar to see if it's trademarked. Again, if it's taken, you'll need to make changes.
   c. **Example**: Carla goes to the US Patent and Trademark Office website and enters "Carla Can Clean" in the TESS search field. She reviews the results and confirms that no similar trademark exists in the same business category. Now that she's checked both the state and federal databases, she knows her chosen business name is fair game.
3. Conduct a domain name verification.
   a. **Check for a matching domain.** Visit a domain registration site (e.g., GoDaddy, Namecheap) and type in your business name to see if a corresponding domain is available.
   b. **Reserve your domain**: If available, it might be a good idea to purchase it immediately to guarantee online brand consistency—and so no one can swoop in and take it while you're waiting around.
   c. **Example**: Carla types "carlacanclean.com" in the domain search field. She finds that it's available, then immediately secures it to set herself up for the future with an online presence that matches her business name.
4. Determine your business's purpose and goals.
   a. **Craft a purpose statement.** Design a focused, to-the-point statement of purpose that can help guide your business as it moves forward.
   b. **Think about what you want out of your business for the future.** Consider all aspects of your business's growth. Sketch your ideas

down so you have something to refer back to.
   c. **Establish a SMART framework and conduct a SWOT analysis.** These serve to lock in goals and methods for yourself to guide you as you develop your LLC.
   d. **Make sure you're considering work-life balance.** If you don't put some focus on taking care of yourself you're going to burn out, so establish clear guidelines for yourself.
   e. **Example**: Carla sketches out her goals for Carla Can Clean LLC, coming up with a purpose statement before focusing on how she wants the business to grow. She then establishes a plan using the SMART framework and conducts a SWOT analysis to make sure she's not missing anything. She also sets aside strict guidelines to make sure she still has plenty of time for her family.
5. Select your LLC's registered agent.
   a. **Choose between an individual or professional service.** Both have their advantages; the former is likely to be cheaper, while the latter comes with a higher guarantee of trustworthiness.
   b. **File the appropriate paperwork to establish your registered agent.** Make sure to double-check for typos or misspellings, as this can slow the process down significantly be necessitating re-filings.
   c. **Example**: Carla considers acting as her own registered agent for Carla Can Clean LLC but ultimately realizes she'd be better served to hire a service for this purpose and enlists professional help. After filing the appropriate

paperwork, she's all good to go. This allows her to focus on the business itself.
6. Create a business plan.
   a. **Choose between an individual or professional service.** Both have their advantages; the former is likely to be cheaper, while the latter comes with a higher guarantee of trustworthiness.
   b. **File the appropriate paperwork to establish your registered agent.** Make sure to double-check for typos or misspellings, as this can slow the process down significantly be necessitating re-filings.
   c. **Example**: Carla considers acting as her own registered agent for Carla Can Clean LLC but ultimately realizes she'd be better served to hire a service for this purpose and enlists professional help. After filing the appropriate paperwork, she's all good to go. This allows her to focus on the business itself.

3
ESTABLISHING YOUR LLC: THE FORMATION PROCESS

Forming your LLC first requires you to file your articles of organization before applying for that EIN we mentioned back in Chapter 1. Let's say that Mia dreams of launching her own artisanal candle company but needs to do this first to finally legitimize her company. Once she gets past her first hurdle of understanding what an articles of organization actually is, she can file that document to register her LLC with the state and grant it legal recognition as a separate entity.

FILING ARTICLES OF ORGANIZATION

The articles of organization is a foundational document that establishes your LLC's existence in the eyes of the state. It is essential for forming an LLC, as it defines each member's liabilities, rights, duties, powers, and other responsibilities surrounding each member of the LLC.

While the information required to fill out the articles of

organization varies by state, certain elements are universally mandatory:

1. **LLC Name and Address:** When filling out the articles of organization, you must provide your company's name and address. Your chosen name must comply with your state's naming rules and include a designation like "LLC" or "Limited Liability Company." You also need to list your LLC's principal place of business.
2. **Registered Agent:** The registered agent's name and address are also required. This individual or entity will be responsible for accepting the delivery of legal documents on behalf of the LLC. The registered agent must have a physical address within the state of formation—PO Boxes are not accepted (Enright 2022).
3. **Purpose of the LLC:** The purpose of the LLC must be stated, although this can often be general, such as "to engage in any lawful activity." A particularly broad purpose like that one is designed to allow flexibility in your business operations. Some states may require a specific purpose, so check with your state's requirements first (Steingold 2024).
4. **Management Structure:** You'll need to provide information on whether your LLC will be member-managed or manager-managed. This will also include information on who the members and managers are. You could also choose to adopt a management structure consisting of a Board of Directors, although this is not typical nor required for an LLC.

Filing Process

Filing the articles of organization requires specific steps, which can vary slightly depending on your state. Most states offer both online and paper filing options, although online filing is often quicker and more convenient. Your state's Secretary of State website will have the forms. Filling it out online is self-explanatory, but paper filing involves downloading the form, filling it out by hand, and mailing it to the appropriate state office. Filing fees vary by state, so be sure to keep aware of yours (we'll get into more details here in Chapter 4). If your state has specific requirements, like publication notices or additional forms, address those to avoid processing delays.

After Filing

After submitting the articles of organization, you'll receive confirmation from the state in the form of a certificate of organization, certificate of formation, or a similar document officially recognizing your LLC. The timeframe for approval can vary, but generally, it takes from a few days to a few weeks, depending on the state and method of filing (SimplifyLLC 2024). Once you receive this confirmation, keep a copy of the filed articles for your records; you'll need this document for opening a business bank account, applying for business licenses, and performing other administrative tasks.

Once all these steps are taken care of, your LLC is legally established and ready to operate. Our example Mia reached this point and found that understanding and completing the articles of organization was a pivotal step in turning her candle-making passion into a thriving business. Now, her LLC protects her personal assets, legitimizes her company in peoples' eyes, and is a solid foundation for growth and success.

GETTING YOUR EIN

With your LLC officially recognized, the next foundational step is obtaining an Employer Identification Number (EIN), which is essential for tax and banking purposes—it's basically the social security number for your business. This federal tax identifier is indispensable for a variety of reasons. First and foremost, you need an EIN to open a business bank account, as financial institutions require an EIN to separate your business and personal finances. Also, if you plan to hire employees in the future, an EIN is mandatory for reporting employment taxes. Even if you choose not to hire employees immediately, you're going to need an EIN eventually for future growth.

The Internal Revenue Service (IRS) provides several methods to apply for an EIN. The quickest and most convenient way is to apply online through the IRS website, a user-friendly process that can be completed in one session. Your EIN is issued immediately upon successful completion, and you can download, save, and print the confirmation notice. Other methods include applying by phone, fax, or mail. Applying by phone involves calling the IRS Business & Specialty Tax Line, while fax and mail applications require filling out Form SS-4 and sending it to the IRS. Fax applications are processed within four business days, while mail applications can take up to four weeks.

To complete the EIN application, you'll need several pieces of information. Start with your LLC's legal name and address, which needs to match the information you provided in your articles of organization. Next, you'll need the principal officer's name and social security number (SSN), often referred to as the "responsible party"; this individual is usually the LLC's managing member or owner. You'll also need to specify the reason for applying for an EIN, and common reasons include "Starting a new business" or "Hiring employees." You'll also need information like the entity type, the date the business was started or acquired, the closing month of the accounting year, and the highest number of people you expect to employ in the next twelve months.

Once you've obtained your EIN, you'll be able to use the EIN for all tax filings related to your LLC, including income, employment, and excise tax returns. You'll also need the EIN when applying for permits and licenses, as many regulatory bodies require it for identification. Make sure to keep the EIN confirmation notice somewhere safe since you'll need to refer back to it for various administrative tasks, and you'll want it to be easily accessible for reference when you need it (Kagan 2024a).

SMOOTH OPERATOR: CREATING AN OPERATING AGREEMENT

The articles of organization isn't the only document you'll need; an operating agreement will ultimately serve as a blueprint for your LLC's management structure and provide clear guidelines for how your business will function. This document, which shows who owns the LLC, is something you might need to refer back to often. Without it, you risk potential disputes, lack of clarity in decision-making, and even legal issues.

While only required in California, Delaware, Maine, Missouri, and New York, I highly recommend creating an operating agreement, especially if the LLC has more than one owner (Prakash 2024). The agreement should clearly outline the roles, responsibilities, and expectations of each member, helping prevent member disputes (should they ever arise). Establishing the LLC's procedures in this document also helps provide legal protection and keeps all members on the same strategic page (Hayes 2024a).

When drafting your Operating Agreement, consider several essential components:

1. **Define Roles and Responsibilities**: Clearly outline each member's role, including their contributions in time, effort, and resources.
2. **Establish Voting Rights and Decision-Making Processes**: Detail how decisions will be made—whether by majority vote, unanimous consent, or another method. This clarity ensures all members understand their voting power and how decisions are reached.
3. **Describe Profit and Loss Distribution**: Specify how profits and losses will be allocated among members. A detailed breakdown can help prevent future disputes over financial matters.
4. **Outline Member Addition and Removal Procedures**: Include the process for adding new members, with any required approvals, and procedures for removing members due to voluntary departure, misconduct, or other reasons.
5. **Define Dissolution Procedures**: Include clear steps for dissolving the LLC, protecting all members' interests, and ensuring an orderly business closure.

If you need help, there are templates and real-world examples of operating agreements available online. These resources can serve as a helpful starting point, giving you a framework around which to customize them for your unique business needs.

Speaking of customization, you're not going to want to simply grab a basic operating agreement template and not make any changes to it because customizing your operating agreement is necessary for it to meet the unique needs of your business. Unsurprisingly, if you have a single-member LLC, your operating agreement will be simpler, focusing on your role as the sole owner. In contrast, a multi-member LLC requires more detailed provisions to address the roles and responsibilities of each member and how decisions will be made collectively. It's also a good idea to include specific clauses relevant to your industry; if you operate in a highly regulated field, for example, you may need to include provisions related to compliance and industry-specific regulations.

When it comes time for Mia to draft her operating agreement, she starts off with a template she finds online. She then customizes it to include specific clauses about sourcing sustainable materials, reflecting her commitment to eco-friendly practices for her candle company. Mia also details the voting process for significant business decisions, making sure all partners have a say in the company's direction. By tailoring her operating agreement to fit the unique needs of her business, Mia creates a framework that guides her company's operations and growth.

> **BONUS:** I have included a fully customizable operating agreement with detailed instructions for you to download in the bonus section.

Creating a detailed and customized operating agreement is an investment in your LLC's future stability and success. By clearly outlining the roles, responsibilities, and procedures, you work to enable smooth operations and effective decision-making. Whether you're a solo entrepreneur or part of a multi-member team, a well-crafted operating agreement provides the structure and clarity needed to successfully run a business.

INITIAL MEMBER CONTRIBUTIONS AND CAPITAL ACCOUNTS

Initial member contributions to your LLC's capital are a necessary part of the process because they establish ownership percentages and financial equity within the company. When forming an LLC, documenting each member's financial or asset contributions is extremely important, as this documentation serves as the basis for determining ownership stakes, directly influencing how profits and losses are distributed. For example, if you and two partners each contribute $10,000, $20,000, and $30,000 respectively, those of you who contributed more initial capital will hold higher ownership percentages, ultimately affecting how earnings are shared. There are no specific legal requirements for how much initial member contributions have to cover, but it's a good idea for them to cover—at a minimum—your business's initial operating costs.

Members can make various types of contributions to the LLC. The most straightforward is cash, where members give the business a set amount of funding. Property or asset contributions are another standard method, and these ultimately have to be valued; one member might contribute office equipment or a vehicle, which can be documented as part of their equity stake (Wong 2024a). Another form of contribution is "sweat equity," where a member offers valuable services—such as legal counsel or marketing expertise—in exchange for ownership interest. Regardless of the type, all contributions must be clearly valued and agreed upon by all members for fairness and transparency (Kenton 2024b).

Accurately documenting and recording member contributions is essential for maintaining clear financial records and avoiding future disputes. Start by drafting contribution agreements that outline the specifics of each member's input, including their contribution's type, value, and ownership percentage; these agreements will serve as formal records for future reference. It's equally important to keep detailed financial records, so use accounting software to track contributions and update the LLC's financial statements regularly. Also, update the operating agreement to reflect any changes in contributions so that it accurately represents the LLC's ownership structure.

Capital accounts, meanwhile, are essential for tracking each member's equity in the LLC. A capital account functions as a ledger, recording each member's initial contributions, additional contributions, distributions, and share of profits and losses. The account's initial balance is based on the member's initial contribution value, and as the business operates, balances adjust to reflect any additional contributions or distributions. For example, if a member initially contributes $10,000 and later adds $5,000, their capital account balance will update to $15,000. Similarly, if $2,000 in profits is distributed to them, this amount will be deducted from their capital account.

Managing capital accounts requires regular adjustments. At the end of each fiscal year, reconcile these accounts to make sure all transactions are accurately recorded and that balances reflect the current equity of each member. This reconciliation process helps identify discrepancies and keeps your financial records accurate and up-to-date for tax reporting and compliance. Accurate capital accounts ultimately provide a clear picture of each member's financial stake, which is essential for filing tax returns and correctly distributing profits and losses (Tuovila 2024).

Understanding and managing initial member contributions and capital accounts is fundamental to your LLC's financial health and transparency. Meticulously documenting contributions, maintaining accurate financial records, and regularly updating capital accounts allows you to keep your operations running smoothly and give every member fair representation. These practices establish a robust financial structure, helping your LLC thrive and grow.

With your LLC's formation process complete and the financial foundation in place, you're ready for the next steps.

ACTION STEPS FOR FORMING YOUR LLC

1. **Prepare and File Your Articles of Organization**
   - Research State Requirements.
   - Complete the Form.
   - Submit and Pay Fees.
2. **Receive and Secure Your Certificate of Organization**
   - Track Filing Status.
   - Obtain and Store Your Certificate.
3. **Apply for an Employer Identification Number (EIN)**
   - Go to the website: https://sa.www4.irs.gov/modiein/individual/index.jsp
   - Click "Begin Application" and complete it within 15 minutes.
   - Save Your EIN Confirmation Notice.
4. **Draft and Finalize Your Operating Agreement (As Necessary)**
5. **Document Member Contributions and Set Up Capital Accounts**
   - Use a spreadsheet or accounting software to keep track of all relevant data.

4
LEGAL AND COMPLIANCE ESSENTIALS

So you've just formed your LLC, and everything seems to be falling into place. Your business name is finalized, your articles of organization are filed, and you've secured your EIN. But it won't be long before you realize maintaining an LLC involves more than just the initial setup. Each state has its own unique regulations and requirements that you need to follow to keep your business in good standing, including annual reports, compliance obligations, and possibly fees.

ANNUAL REPORTS AND ONGOING COMPLIANCE OBLIGATIONS

When running an LLC, one of the ongoing tasks you'll need to manage is submitting annual reports, which serve to confirm your LLC's current status with the state. This confirmation keeps your business in good standing and makes sure all public records are up-to-date. Typically, annual reports include basic but essential information such as the names and addresses of your LLC's members or managers and the LLC's principal place of business. Updating this information annually helps maintain transparency and keeps your business compliant with state regulations.

Filing an annual report may sound intimidating, but once you understand the steps involved, it's a pretty straightforward process. Most states offer online filing options on their business filing website, so you can generally submit your report from anywhere. Complete the form by filling in the requested information, such as your LLC's name, registered agent details, and the names and addresses of members or managers. If your state offers a paper filing option, you also can download the form, fill it out manually, and mail it to the provided address—just be sure to include the required filing fee, which varies by state. In some cases, you might need additional documentation like financial statements or proof of compliance with other state regulations.

Beyond annual reports, there are other ongoing compliance obligations you need to deal with to keep your LLC in good standing. One of these is paying state franchise taxes, state-imposed fees for the privilege of operating as an LLC and due annually or biennially (depending on your state's requirements). The calculation methods for franchise taxes can vary; some states base the amount on your LLC's income or asset value, while others use a flat rate (Hayes 2024b). You also have to renew your business licenses and permits regularly. Renewal schedules differ, and there are far too many potential options to go over them here, so you'll have to track these dates for yourself.

Non-compliance with these ongoing obligations can have serious repercussions for your LLC. Missing deadlines for filing annual reports or paying franchise taxes can result in late fees and penalties—or it can even lead to the suspension of your LLC's good standing status, causing you difficulties in securing loans, entering contracts, or expanding your business. In extreme cases, prolonged noncompliance can result in administrative dissolution, where the state revokes your LLC's legal status entirely. This dissolution means your LLC ceases to exist, and you lose the liability protection it provides, exposing your personal assets to potential risks (Payne n.d.).

Beneficial Ownership Reporting Requirement for 2024 and Beyond

Starting in 2024, a new federal requirement mandates LLCs and corporations to file a Beneficial Owner Information (BOI) Report with the Financial Crimes Enforcement Network (FinCEN n.d.). This regulation applies to most businesses, with the goal of increasing transparency and combating illicit activities such as money laundering and fraud.

For businesses registered **before January 1, 2024**, the deadline to submit the BOI report is **January 1, 2025**. Companies formed or registered between **January 1, 2024** through **December 31, 2024**, have 90 days from the date you received the notice of the company's effective registration from the state in which you filed. Companies formed **on or after January 1, 2024**, must file their BOI report within **30 days** of receiving their notice of registration or creation.

This report requires identifying information about the individuals who own or control the company in order to keep compliance with federal guidelines. In the Department of the Treasury's own words, the goal is that this regulation "will eliminate critical vulnerabilities in our financial system and allow us to tackle the scourge of illicit finance enabled by opaque corporate structures" (US Department of the Treasury 2024).

To learn more about the BOI requirements or to submit your report, visit the official FinCEN website: fincen.gov/boi.

Failing to comply with BOI reporting requirements can result in significant consequences, including civil and criminal penalties. Companies that fail to file on time or submit incorrect information may face fines of up to **$591 per day** until the issue is resolved. Willful non-compliance or providing fraudulent information can lead to fines of up to **$10,000** or imprisonment for up to **two years**.

> NOTE: On December 26, 2024, BOI reporting was placed on pause due to a federal court of appeals blocking the reporting deadline. All small business owners should still remain ready to file BOI reports, until the court says otherwise. As of now, it is not required; however, stay prepared, consider voluntary filing, and monitor updates on the FinCEN website.

Understanding and managing your LLC's annual reports and other compliance obligations is extremely important for maintaining your business's legal standing and operational efficiency. By staying on top of these requirements, you avoid the worst-case legal scenarios for your business.

UNDERSTANDING STATE-SPECIFIC LLC REQUIREMENTS

As I've noted, each state has its own regulations that govern LLCs, which can vary significantly. Since these can impact everything from how you form your LLC to how you maintain it over time, you're going to need to know what yours are. One of the first differences you'll notice is the variability in formation fees. Some states have relatively low fees, making it affordable to start an LLC—others, though, have higher fees, which run a lot higher. Forming an LLC in Montana, for example, will cost $35, whereas it could be as high as $500 in Massachusetts. These fees are just the beginning, as ongoing costs like annual fees and franchise taxes vary by state. For example, California filing fees will run you $70, but you'll have to pay a yearly tax fee of $800 (plus a biannual fee of $20) to the franchise tax board (Horwitz 2024).

You need to make sure you're getting accurate state-specific information in order to guarantee you're following the law. Your state government's website, typically managed by the Secretary of State or a similar office, should have what you need. These websites often provide comprehensive resources, including guidelines, forms, and FAQs tailored to LLCs. Online legal resources and databases can also be helpful here, as they offer detailed explanations and up-to-date information on state-specific regulations. If you're unsure about any requirements, contacting your state's business registration office directly is a good idea.

Reporting requirements also differ, in many cases pretty significantly. Some states require detailed annual reports with extensive information about your LLC's activities and financial status. Others have more straightforward reporting requirements, focusing on basic information like the names and addresses of members and managers. California mandates a detailed Statement of Information filed with the Secretary of State every two years, while Arizona has no annual reporting requirement at all.

Annual report filing deadlines can vary widely by state, too—and as we've talked about, you don't want to miss deadlines. You also have to consider publication requirements, with some states mandating that you publish a notice of your LLC's formation in a local newspaper. New York is a prime example, as it requires an announcement in two newspapers for six consecutive weeks (Odegard 2018).

Fortunately, there are plenty of online data bases for such a thing. I've also put together a guide to link you directly to your state and makes it easy to track requirements by state. See the Bonus Section to download: *The Ultimate State-by-State LLC Formation Guide: Filing Fees, Annual Taxes & Official Links for All 50 States, Washington D.C., and U.S. Territories.*

You'll want to make use of that guide, too, because failing to adhere to state-specific requirements can have serious consequences. In addition to the penalties, fines, and potential dissolution we already discussed, non-compliance can damage your business credibility, making it difficult to secure financing, attract customers, or enter into contracts well into the future, even after the issue is resolved.

Checklist: State-Specific Compliance

- **Research state regulations.** Start with your state's government website for specific

guidelines (or use one of the databases that keep track of this info).
- **Check formation fees.** Make sure you understand the initial and ongoing costs for your state.
- **Understand reporting requirements.** Know what information you must report annually or biennially.
- **Maintain records.** Keep copies of all filings and confirmations for future reference.

By understanding and adhering to your state's specific requirements, you can maintain your LLC's good standing and avoid unnecessary legal complications. This diligence protects your business and allows you to focus on the actual work of developing and growing it.

UNDERSTANDING AND MANAGING BUSINESS LICENSES AND PERMITS

We've talked about permits and licenses some, but it's time to dig deeper into what they actually are and how they work. When you start an LLC, securing the proper business licenses and permits is a necessity since they're essential for legal operations. These permits validate your company in the eyes of the law, enhancing your credibility and allowing you to focus on growth without the looming fear of legal repercussions.

The types of licenses and permits you may need can vary widely depending on your industry and location. A general business license, which allows you to conduct business activities within your city or county, is pretty standard. Health and safety permits, meanwhile, are a necessity if your business involves food preparation, healthcare, or any activity that impacts public health in order to keep your operations in line with necessary health and safety standards. Zoning permits are another common requirement, especially if you plan to operate a home-based business or open a physical storefront. These permits confirm that your business activities comply with local zoning laws, which dictate how land in certain areas can be used (Maverick 2024).

Applying for these licenses and permits can be a multi-step process. Your city or county government website should have detailed information on the necessary local requirements for your specific business type, as well as the application process. You'll also need to complete application forms, which typically ask for basic details about your business, such as its name, address, and the nature of its activities. If you're applying for a home-based business permit, for example, the form might require details about the type of business, the expected number of visitors, and any modifications to your home. Once you've filled out the forms, submit them along with any required fees. Some permits may also require inspections or approvals from various agencies before they're granted, so make sure to double-check your specific situation.

As we touched on in previous chapters, permits also require renewal and ongoing maintenance. Depending on local regulations, many licenses and permits must be renewed annually or every two years. Missing these renewal deadlines can lead to fines or the suspension of your business activities, so make sure to set reminders so you don't miss deadlines. Take the time to keep thorough records of all your licenses and permits so you can refer back to them when you need to, storing them in a safe and accessible place.

Checklist: Applying for Business Licenses and Permits

- **Research Local Requirements**: Start with your city or county government website.
- **Complete Application Forms**: Provide all requested information about your business.
- **Submit Forms and Fees**: Ensure all documents are submitted correctly and on time.
- **Schedule Inspections**: If required, arrange for any necessary inspections.
- **Keep Records**: Store your licenses and permits safely and track renewal dates.

COMMON LEGAL PITFALLS AND HOW TO AVOID THEM

Running an LLC comes with its share of legal pitfalls that can jeopardize your business if you don't carefully manage them. One of the most common mistakes is mixing personal and business finances. Many new LLC owners fall into this trap, thinking using personal accounts for business transactions is harmless. The problem is doing this can lead to the loss of liability protection, making your personal assets vulnerable in case of legal actions against your LLC.

Failing to follow the operating agreement is another common error. We've talked about the importance of operating agreements, but it's important to understand that ignoring them can cause internal conflicts and undermine your business's legal standing. For example, if LLC members include an annual meeting requirement in their operating agreement, then adhering to that requirement is legally necessary. Not properly documenting meetings and decisions also risks disputes among members and legal complications without proper records, especially if the business faces litigation (Porter n.d.).

Maintaining separate bank accounts for your LLC helps you steer clear of these pitfalls, as it preserves your limited liability status and simplifies accounting and tax filing. Run all business transactions through your LLC's bank account and resist the urge to use personal funds for business expenses. Adhering strictly to the operating agreement's provisions and following them diligently helps maintain order and legal compliance.

So, what's the best way to keep everything in order? It's simple: proper documentation of anything that might be important for your business. Record-keeping that documents all member contributions and distributions is the best way to keep transparency and fairness among members, preventing future disputes over financial matters. Keeping records of all major business decisions—whether it's entering into a significant contract, taking on a new partner, or making a substantial investment—provides clarity and legal protection. Regularly updating the operating agreement matters, too—as your business grows and changes, this document needs to grow and change with it, accurately reflecting any changes in management, member roles, or operational procedures.

UTILIZING PROFESSIONAL SERVICES: WHEN TO CONSULT AN ATTORNEY OR ACCOUNTANT

Running an LLC can involve a lot of tricky legal and financial matters, and it's completely understandable if a lot of them feel incomprehensible to a layperson. In these situations, consulting professionals such as attorneys and accountants can be invaluable. Both can keep you in compliance with state and federal laws—which, as we've established, is how you avoid legal quagmires. Attorneys can help draft and review legal documents, guaranteeing they are airtight and serve to protect your interests. Accountants, meanwhile, can optimize tax strategies, helping you save money and stay in line with tax regulations. Their expertise can be particularly beneficial during tax season, audits, or when you're making significant financial decisions.

There are specific scenarios where professional help becomes more or less necessary, and the aforementioned tax situations or audits are a particularly good example. If your LLC's financial dealings are intricate, an accountant can help you avoid particularly costly mistakes. There are times you'll really want an attorney, too, such as disputes among LLC members. Legal counsel can mediate conflicts, draft agreements, and keep all parties cognizant of their rights and responsibilities. Major transactions like mergers or acquisitions, meanwhile, are a good time to have both accountants and lawyers on board since they tend to involve a mixture of issues surrounding detailed contracts, financial scrutiny, and regulatory compliance.

When selecting the right professionals, you want to make sure you're making an informed decision. Start by checking the credentials and experience of anyone whose services you're considering employing, making sure the attorney or accountant you choose has relevant qualifications and a track record of working with LLCs specifically. Reading reviews and seeking recommendations from other business owners can be helpful, and personal referrals often lead you to trusted professionals who have proven their expertise to people whose opinions you value. You probably shouldn't just pick one immediately; interviewing multiple candidates is generally a good call. Discuss your specific needs, ask about their experience with similar businesses, and gauge their understanding of your industry. Taking your time with this process helps you find a professional who has the right skills and fits well with your business ethos and communication style.

Understanding the cost versus benefit of professional services matters a lot. While hiring an attorney or accountant may seem like an additional expense, it can save you a lot of money and headaches in the long run by getting out in front of legal and issues that might otherwise result in costly lawsuits and penalties. An accountant's expertise in tax planning, meanwhile, can lead to significant tax savings, outweighing their fees. Moreover, professionals can handle complex tasks more efficiently than you're likely to, allowing you to focus on growing your business. The peace of mind that comes from knowing your LLC is compliant with all legal and financial regulations is invaluable because you don't have to think about any of this.

5

TAX STRATEGIES AND BENEFITS

You're probably going to be excited when you receive your first significant payment from a client. And why wouldn't you? It's a job well done and time to reap the spoils of your hard-earned work.

Not so fast, though, because this money isn't entirely yours—well, not all of it, anyway. You need to pay taxes on it, and as an LLC owner, understanding your tax obligations is as important as it is complex. Taxes can be a pain in the behind, but with the proper knowledge and tools, you can manage your LLC's taxes efficiently and even take advantage of tax benefits, turning the financial ballgame in your favor.

TAXATION BASICS FOR LLCS: WHAT YOU NEED TO KNOW

Understanding the tax obligations for your LLC starts with knowing how your business structure affects your tax treatment. If you operate a single-member LLC, the

IRS treats it as a sole proprietorship by default. It is considered a "disregarded entity" where all profits and losses from the business are reported on your personal income tax return, specifically on Schedule C of Form 1040. This process simplifies tax filing but still requires meticulous record-keeping to keep things accurate.

For multi-member LLCs, meanwhile, the IRS defaults to regarding the entity as a partnership. In this case, the LLC itself does not pay federal income taxes; instead, profits and losses pass through to the members, who report them on their personal tax returns using Schedule K-1. The LLC must also file Form 1065, an informational return that outlines the business's financial performance (Simons 2024).

The types of taxes your LLC must pay can vary, but several common obligations exist. Federal income tax is a big concern, and how it's calculated depends on your LLC's tax classification. Single-member LLCs report business income on the owner's personal tax return (Internal Revenue Service 2024a), while multi-member LLCs distribute income to members, who then report it individually (Internal Revenue Service 2024b).

You might also need to pay state income tax, depending on where your LLC operates. Each state has different rules and rates, so it's essential to understand your state's specific requirements. Self-employment taxes—which include Social Security and Medicare contributions—are another significant obligation; as an LLC owner, you're responsible for both the employer and employee portions, which can add up to a substantial amount. Additionally, if your business sells goods or services, you may need to collect sales tax from customers and remit it to the state. The rate and rules for sales tax vary by state and sometimes by locality, so you're going to have to do the legwork to find all of this out on state websites.

As mentioned above, keeping accurate financial records is going to make this whole process a whole lot easier. Accounting software is great for tracking all income and expenses meticulously, and it can generate reports that simplify tax filing and help identify deductible expenses. One accounting tool I recommend is Zoho Books, as they have a free starter plan (Yakal 2024a). As you grow your company and have more transactions and bills, upgrading to a different plan or a more advanced tool like Intuit QuickBooks would be ideal for your needs (Yakal 2024b).

You'll also need to make estimated tax payments to avoid running afoul of the law. The IRS requires you to pay taxes on income as you earn it, which means making quarterly estimated tax payments if you expect to owe $1,000 or more in taxes when you file your return. These payments help you avoid penalties for underpayment. To calculate your estimated tax amounts, use Form 1040-ES, which provides worksheets to help you estimate your tax liability for the year (Internal Revenue Service 2024c). Since these are due quarterly, it's a good idea to set aside funds throughout the year for these payments; a separate savings account for tax funds can be helpful to make sure you have the necessary amount available when payments are due.

UNDERSTANDING PASS-THROUGH TAXATION AND ITS BENEFITS

As mentioned way back in Chapter 1, pass-through taxation is one of the most significant advantages of forming an LLC. As a refresher: Pass-through taxation means that the business itself does not pay federal income taxes. Instead, the income generated by the LLC "passes through" to the individual members, who then report this income on their personal tax returns. While corporations deal with double taxation, where both the business and the shareholders pay taxes on the same income, LLCs face taxation only once.

Those are the basics, but the benefits of pass-through taxation are numerous even beyond just paying taxes once rather than twice. First, it simplifies tax filing: Unlike corporations that must file separate corporate tax returns, LLCs allow you to report business income and expenses directly on your personal tax return. This structure reduces the paperwork and complexity involved in tax preparation. Additionally, pass-through taxation allows you to deduct legitimate business expenses such as rent, utilities, salaries, and office supplies, reducing your taxable income and thereby lowering your tax bill even further.

To illustrate how pass-through taxation applies, let's use the hypothetical example of a single-member LLC owned by Sarah. At the end of the year, Sarah's LLC generates a profit of $50,000. Because her LLC is treated as a sole proprietorship for tax purposes, she reports this income on her personal tax return using Schedule C. She can also deduct business expenses, such as $5,000 for office rent and $3,000 for supplies, lowering her overall taxable income.

In contrast, a multi-member LLC like Tech Innovators (again, not a real company!), owned by Alex and Jamie, generates $100,000 in profit. This profit is split between them based on their ownership percentages—say 60 percent for Alex and 40 percent for Jamie. Each member receives a Schedule K-1, which details their share of the income. Alex reports $60,000, and Jamie reports $40,000. This structure keeps the income from being taxed twice, as would a corporation.

While pass-through taxation offers many advantages, you also need to understand its potential drawbacks, because there are a few. One is that the income is taxed at all the members' personal income tax rates, so your tax liability could be substantial if you fall into a high tax bracket. Additionally, pass-through income is subject to self-employment tax, which includes Social Security and Medicare contributions, which can add up, especially for high earners. If Sarah from our earlier example is in the 24 percent tax bracket, her $50,000 profit (less expenses) will be taxed at this rate on top of her self-employment tax—a considerable amount (Woodside 2024b).

Understanding these nuances helps you make informed decisions about your LLC's tax strategy. While the simplicity and potential savings of pass-through taxation are appealing, it's important to think about your overall tax situation and possibly consult with a tax professional to make sure you're maximizing the benefits of your LLC's tax structure while minimizing any drawbacks.

ELECTING S-CORP STATUS: PROS, CONS, AND PROCESS

Understanding how S-Corporation status works can significantly impact your LLC's tax strategy and overall financial health. As we mentioned back in Chapter 1, you can elect to have your LLC treated as an S-Corp—but what does that actually mean?

In brief, an S-Corporation election allows your LLC to be taxed as an S-Corp while retaining the LLC's legal structure, a particularly relevant choice for LLCs looking to optimize their tax situation. To qualify, your LLC must meet specific eligibility criteria: It must be a domestic entity, have no more than 100 shareholders, and have only one class of stock. Unlike a C-Corp, an S-Corp does not face double taxation, meaning the corporation does not pay federal income tax. Instead, income, losses, deductions, and credits pass through to shareholders to be reported on their individual tax returns.

Electing S-Corp status offers several advantages that can be pretty beneficial, such as the potential savings on self-employment taxes. In a standard LLC, all profits are subject to self-employment tax, but with an S-Corp election, only the salaries paid to owners are subject to this levy, and the remaining profits are distributed as dividends. This structure can lead to significant tax savings, primarily if your LLC generates substantial income. Additionally, S-Corp status allows for continued pass-through taxation benefits, meaning the business's income is only taxed once individually. Salary and distribution structures also possess quite a bit of flexibility, as you can pay yourself a reasonable salary and take additional profits as distributions, optimizing your tax liabilities.

You have to weigh these benefits against the potential downsides of S-Corp status, though. One of the primary disadvantages is the increased complexity of tax filing and compliance since an S-Corp must file Form 1120S, an additional tax return, and meet stricter IRS guidelines. This requirement adds a layer of administrative work and may necessitate hiring a tax professional just to get everything filed correctly. Another drawback is the restrictions on ownership and stock classes: An S-Corp cannot have more than 100 shareholders, and all shareholders must be US citizens or residents. If you have a single foreign national as a shareholder, S-Corp status is off the table. Additionally, S-Corps can only issue one class of stock, which can limit your ability to attract different types of investors. The last downside gets back to that salary and distribution structure, which it turns out is something of a double-edged sword: The IRS requires that owners pay themselves a "reasonable salary" before taking distributions. This mandate can complicate payroll and requires careful documentation to avoid IRS scrutiny.

If you decide that the benefits outweigh the drawbacks, electing S-Corp status involves several steps. First, you need to file Form 2553, "Election by a Small Business Corporation," with the IRS within seventy-five days of forming your LLC or the start of the tax year in which you want the election to take effect. The form requires basic information about your LLC, including its name, address, and the names of all shareholders, and each shareholder must also sign it, indicating their consent to the election. Once the form is submitted and approved, your LLC will be treated as an S-Corp for tax purposes.

After electing S-Corp status, ongoing compliance and reporting requirements are just as important as they are for everything else. Maintaining accurate records is a must, and all shareholders have to be paid reasonable salaries, so you'll have to set up a payroll system and withhold the appropriate taxes. Additionally, you must file Form 1120S annually, along with Schedule K-1 for each shareholder, detailing their share of the income, deductions, and credits. It's a fair amount of paperwork—but to be fair, so is pretty much everything when it comes to business accounting (Nelson 2024).

By understanding the intricacies of S-Corp status, you can make an informed decision that matches your LLC's financial goals and operational needs. While the process may seem complex, the potential tax savings and operational flexibility can provide significant advantages for your business over both the short and long term.

ADVANCED TAX STRATEGIES FOR LLC OWNERS

There's a lot to think about with taxes, so it would behoove you to think about as much of it as possible ahead of time. Proactive tax planning is thus a very important aspect of running a successful LLC; by planning ahead, you can maximize your tax savings and keep from the wrong side of what can sometimes seem like ever-changing tax laws. Hiring a professional is a good idea, but even if you do, you should still try to stay informed about tax law changes yourself. Subscribe to tax newsletters, attend webinars, read relevant publications—whatever you can do to keep your knowledge current. If you're doing it right, this dual approach means you're well-prepared for tax season and can even capitalize on potential savings.

About those savings—let's go over a couple. Income splitting is a powerful strategy that significantly reduces your overall tax liability. By allocating income to family members in lower tax brackets, you can lower the total tax paid by your household. This method involves either paying salaries to family members who work in your business or setting up family partnerships. For example, if you have a spouse or adult children who contribute to the business, paying them a reasonable salary can shift income from your higher tax bracket to their lower one—

and it's completely legal (Kagan 2020). Utilizing trusts can also be effective since placing business assets in a trust allows you to control how income is distributed, further optimizing your tax situation.

Setting up retirement plans for your LLC offers both tax benefits and long-term financial security. Plans like SEP-IRA, SIMPLE IRA, and Solo 401(k) are tailored for small businesses and provide significant advantages. A SEP-IRA allows you to contribute up to 25 percent of your net earnings, with a maximum limit of $69,000 for 2024, which will increase to $70,000 in 2025. Contributions are tax-deductible, lowering your taxable income. A SIMPLE IRA, meanwhile, is easier to set up and administer, with contribution limits of $13,500 plus an additional $3,000 for those over fifty. The Solo 401(k) is ideal for business owners with no employees, offering high contribution limits and the ability to make both employer and employee contributions. Employee contributions in 2024 cap at $23,000 but will increase to $23,500 in 2025. These plans can do wonders to both reduce your current tax liability and help secure your financial future (Ayoola 2024).

Several tax credits and deductions are available to LLCs, each designed to lower your taxable income and reduce your overall tax bill. The home office deduction allows you to deduct expenses related to the business use of your home. This typically means a portion of your rent or mortgage, utilities, and maintenance, based on the percentage of your home dedicated for work purposes (Orem 2024). Section 179 expensing lets you deduct the full cost of qualifying equipment and software purchased for your business up to a limit of $1,220,000 for 2024 for taxes filed in 2025. This deduction is particularly beneficial for businesses making significant capital investments (Hayes

2024c). The research and development tax credit, meanwhile, rewards businesses that invest in innovation. If your LLC is involved in developing new products, processes, or software, you can claim this credit to offset a portion of your research expenses (Karamon et al. 2024). Lastly, the small business healthcare tax credit is available to businesses that provide health insurance to their employees. This credit can cover a significant portion of your healthcare costs, making it more affordable to offer competitive employee benefits (Internal Revenue Service 2024d).

You also need to worry about accurately managing self-employment taxes. For the reasons outlined above, an S-Corp election can help with this, but it's not the only way to be proactive here, as maximizing deductible business expenses is also essential. Keep detailed records of all business-related expenses, such as travel, meals, and supplies, to allow yourself to claim all eligible deductions. If you pay for health insurance premiums, you can also deduct these costs, provided you meet specific IRS requirements (Henricks 2024).

Real-world hypothetical examples illustrate how these advanced tax strategies can lead to substantial savings. Let's say there's an LLC owner named Kevin who implemented income splitting by paying a salary to a spouse working in the business. This strategy shifted a significant portion of Kevin's income to a lower tax bracket, reducing the overall tax bill. Another example could involve an LLC owner named Melissa, who set up a Solo 401(k) and made maximum contributions. These contributions were tax-deductible, lowering Melissa's taxable income and providing a solid retirement savings plan.

Incorporating these advanced tax strategies can ultimately optimize your LLC's financial health and set you up for long-term success. Proactive tax planning, income splitting, retirement plans, and effective management of self-employment taxes are powerful tools that can significantly impact your bottom line as long as you deploy them correctly. Understanding and implementing these strategies can save you quite a bit of money and provide peace of mind, knowing your LLC is financially optimized and you're not going to run on the wrong side of any tax laws.

SUCCESS: A SHIFT IN PERSPECTIVE

"To succeed in business, to reach the top, an individual must know all it is possible to know about the business." – J. Paul Getty

Let me take you back to the conversation I had with my friend Dean at the beginning of this book. Dean had been successful in setting up an LLC, but when I asked him why he chose to do so, his answer revealed something I've encountered often. While he knew about a few of the advantages his decision was largely influenced by what others told him was the "best option."

I think about that conversation all the time because it highlights a challenge many entrepreneurs face. They recognize that an LLC is important but don't always understand how to use it strategically. All too often, business owners stop at formation, missing opportunities to grow, protect, and elevate their business. The truth is, success isn't just about following a checklist—it's about understanding the "why" behind each step and using that knowledge to your advantage. This book is designed to help you shift your perspective, giving you the clarity to see how your LLC fits into the broader vision of your business.

It's become my mission to help aspiring business owners start their LLC with this shift in perspective. It really is a great option, but only if you understand how to use it to your advantage—and I hope that's something you're beginning to get a better idea of now.

By leaving a review of this book on Amazon, you'll help new readers find this book, and you'll inspire them to set out on their LLC journey with a clear understanding of the steps head.

When we approach business with the right perspective—knowing not just what to do but why—we open the door to greater success. That's the shift I want every entrepreneur to experience, and your support can help make it possible for others.

Thank you so much for your support. I know it doesn't seem like much, but it makes a huge difference.

Scan the QR code below:

6

FINANCIAL MANAGEMENT

If there's a single aspect of operating an LLC that requires the most time and attention, even more than keeping up with official documentation, it's probably financial management. Among the many challenges new LLC owners face, financial management is one of the most important—and potentially overwhelming—tasks. From setting up dedicated bank accounts to selecting the right accounting software, you absolutely cannot overlook getting the financial management aspect of your business right. Luckily, there are plenty of tricks to lean on in order to get the most out of your efforts.

SETTING UP YOUR LLC'S BANK ACCOUNTS AND FINANCIAL SYSTEMS

One of the first and most important steps in managing your LLC's finances is setting up separate bank accounts for your business. Keeping personal and business finances separate is essential for maintaining the legal protection afforded by your LLC, as by keeping your business transactions distinct from personal ones, you protect your personal assets in case of legal issues. If your LLC faces a lawsuit or incurs debt, having separate accounts helps keep your personal property safe. It has the added bonus of simplifying tax preparation and financial tracking because when tax season arrives, having all business transactions in one place makes it easier to pull together the necessary information for your paperwork. Lastly, it signals professionalism and credibility to your clients and vendors, showing them you run your business with diligence and integrity (Bank of America 2024).

Choosing the right bank for your LLC involves thinking about several factors that match your business needs. First, look for a bank that offers comprehensive business banking services, including basic checking and savings accounts, as well as more advanced options like business loans and lines of credit. Fees and account maintenance costs are another thing to consider: Some banks charge monthly fees or require a minimum balance to avoid these charges, so if possible, opt for a bank that offers reasonable fees and favorable terms. The availability of online banking and mobile app capabilities is also essential, as the modern world requires being able to manage your finances on the go, and features like mobile check deposit, online bill pay, and real-time transaction alerts can significantly enhance your financial management.

Opening a business bank account is a simple process, but it does require specific documentation. As usual, you'll need a bunch of documents including your LLC's EIN, articles of organization, and operating agreement. These documents verify your business's legal standing, and they'll help the bank set up your account correctly. Depending on the bank, you might need to go in person, but you might also have the option to set up the account online. You'll usually need an initial deposit to open the account, which varies by bank. After setting up your account, take advantage of the bank's online banking services and set up online banking to monitor your account, make electronic transfers, and pay bills. Payment processing services might also be a good idea if your business accepts credit card payments, as it can help enable smooth transactions and make sure you get paid quickly.

Efficient financial management also involves using the right tools and software, so don't leave the technology side of things by the wayside. Accounting software can help you track income and expenses, generate financial reports, and simplify tax preparation. As mentioned in Chapter 5, I highly recommend Intuit QuickBooks for small businesses due to its comprehensive features, including inventory management, time tracking, and customizable reports (Yakal 2024b). FreshBooks is another excellent option, especially for very small businesses, as it offers a smooth user experience and strong invoicing capabilities (Crawford 2024). Implementing accounting software early on can save you time and reduce errors, allowing you to focus on growing your business without worrying nearly as much about your financial maintenance situation.

Incorporating these financial systems and practices into your daily operations sets a solid foundation for your LLC's success. Keeping your finances organized, using the right tools, and maintaining clear records keeps your LLC running smoothly and compliant with all financial regulations. Doing diligence ahead of the game helps protect your business and positions it for sustained growth and profitability.

HANDLING BUSINESS DEBT AND CREDIT

One of the things about owning a business that might surprise people who've never done it is you're likely to deal with debt as a major issue, at least at the start of your business's life. Effectively managing business debt is thus extremely important for the financial health of your LLC. One of the smartest moves is to prioritize high-interest debt repayment; high interest rates can quickly escalate the amount you owe, making it harder to pay off over time. Focusing on these debts first reduces the overall interest you pay, freeing up cash flow for other business needs.

Another strategy is to negotiate with creditors directly. Many creditors are willing to work with you to create a more manageable repayment plan, especially if it means they'll eventually see the money they're owed. You can often negotiate lower interest rates, extended payment terms, or even a reduction in the total amount owed. Open communication with creditors can create favorable terms that help your LLC stay financially stable, so don't just assume you know what they'll say (and that it will be *"nuh uh,* pay us").

You'll want to prioritize both of these strategies because maintaining good credit is essential for your LLC's growth and financial opportunities. A strong credit history can open doors to better financing options, lower interest rates, and favorable terms with suppliers—and it looks good to anyone you'd like to work with. The simplest part of building a strong credit history is also the exact one you'd expect: Pay all business bills and debts on time, as doing so is a significant factor in determining your credit score. Regularly monitoring your credit reports is also important, so be sure to check for inaccuracies or discrepancies that could negatively impact your score and address them promptly.

Improving your business credit score itself also involves several steps, such as establishing credit with companies reporting trade information and lowering your credit utilization. Utilizing a business credit card responsibly and paying off balances in full each month is a good idea. Sometimes, leveraging business credit cards with an introductory period of 0% APY—even if you don't actually need the credit to pay for anything—can help until your business has a positive cash flow. I've applied for several business cards, charged business expenses, and then paid them off before the interest starts to kick in after the first year.

Sometimes, you do need the credit to pay for things, though, and securing business financing is often necessary for supporting your operations and growth. To obtain a loan, you should definitely prepare a strong business plan, as a well-drafted business plan demonstrates to lenders that you have a clear strategy for growth and the ability to repay the loan. It should include financial projections, market analysis, and details about your management team. Exploring various financing options is also a smart idea; traditional bank loans, small business administration (SBA) loans, and alternative financing options like online lenders or crowdfunding—or some combination thereof—can provide the necessary capital. Applying for an SBA loan is a particularly attractive option, as these loans often come with lower interest rates and longer repayment terms. They do, however, require thorough documentation and a strong business plan for you to qualify for them (Murphy and Kris 2024).

Maintaining financial stability involves careful cash flow management and planning for unexpected expenses. Creating a budget helps you plan for expenses, manage cash flow, and identify areas where you can cut costs. Of course, you'll have to stick to that budget so you don't overspend and so you can allocate funds efficiently. Setting aside reserves for emergencies is also a good idea, as unforeseen expenses can hit you at any time, and having a financial cushion can keep your business afloat during tough times. Aim to build an emergency fund that covers at least three to six months of operating expenses; a reserve can provide you with both financial security and peace of mind.

BUDGETING AND FINANCIAL PLANNING FOR YOUR LLC

We just mentioned how creating a budget is a good idea, but let's dive a little deeper. A well-crafted budget helps you plan for expenses, manage cash flow, and set financial goals, allowing you to identify areas where you can cut costs, allocate resources more efficiently, and set benchmarks to measure your financial performance. By having a clear financial plan, you know exactly where your money is going, which allows you to make informed decisions that align with your business objectives.

An effective budget consists of several key components. Start with revenue projections; based on market research and historical data, estimate how much income your business will generate over a specific period. This forecast should take into account seasonal fluctuations, market trends, and potential new revenue streams. Next, break down your expenses into fixed and variable categories. Fixed expenses are regular, recurring costs like rent, salaries, and insurance premiums, while variable expenses fluctuate and can include marketing costs, utility bills, and raw materials. There are also personnel costs to consider like marketing efforts and employee salaries. Additionally, it's essential to set aside contingency funds for unexpected costs. These reserves act as a financial cushion, helping you deal with unforeseen expenses without disrupting your overall budget.

You're also going to want to make sure your ambitions don't exceed your reach. It's good to aim high, but in the short term, you also have to be realistic. Set clear financial goals and milestones, both short-term and long-term—objectives like reaching a specific revenue target, expanding your product line, or entering new markets. Having defined milestones helps you track your progress and stay focused on your objectives.

Regularly reviewing and adjusting your budget is necessary to stay on track, too. Conduct monthly or quarterly budget reviews to compare actual figures against your projections and analyze any variances between projected and actual numbers to understand the reasons behind them. This helps you identify trends, spot potential issues early on, and make data-driven adjustments to your spending and investment strategies. If you notice that your marketing expenses are consistently higher than budgeted, for example, you might need to reevaluate your marketing strategy or find ways to optimize your spending.

Incorporating these budgeting and financial planning practices sets a solid foundation for your LLC's financial health. A detailed budget helps you manage day-to-day expenses and provides a strategic framework for long-term growth while regularly monitoring and adjusting your budget. The budget you create allows you to adapt to changes, seize opportunities, and deal with challenges effectively. This proactive approach to financial management empowers you to make informed decisions, optimize your resources, and confidently achieve your business goals.

UNDERSTANDING AND PREPARING FINANCIAL STATEMENTS

Financial statements are another part of being a business owner since they're the backbone of your financial reporting, providing a clear picture of your business's performance and financial health. The income statement, also known as the profit and loss statement, summarizes your revenues, costs, and expenses over a specific period—ultimately giving a snapshot of whether your business is profitable or not. It also lists your assets, liabilities, and equity, illustrating what your business owns and owes. Finally, the cash flow statement tracks the flow of cash in and out of your business, detailing operational, investing, and financing activities. This helps you understand how well your business generates cash to meet its debt obligations and fund its operating expenses (C. Murphy 2024).

Creating accurate financial statements starts with gathering all financial data, including sales records, expense receipts, bank statements, and payroll records. Next, use accounting software to compile and organize this data. Tools I've already mentioned like QuickBooks Online or FreshBooks can streamline this task, automating calculations and generating reports. Input all your financial transactions into the software, categorizing them appropriately. It will then help you generate the income statement, balance sheet, and cash flow statement. You're going to want to regularly update your financial data to allow for current and precise financial statements.

Accurate financial reporting is a powerful tool for decision-making, but it also makes you look good in the eyes of anyone you might need to work with. Precision in financial statements supports loan applications for one thing by showing lenders a clear and reliable picture of your business's financial health. Investors, meanwhile, also rely on these documents to assess the viability and profitability of your business. Accurate reports build trust and credibility for your business, which are essential for securing funding and investment. Furthermore, precise financial reporting helps you make informed business decisions, such as when to expand, cut costs, or invest in new opportunities. It provides a factual basis for strategic planning and performance evaluation, keeping your decisions grounded in reality.

Analyzing your own financial statements can also provide deep insights into your business's performance and potential areas for improvement. Examining the income statement allows you to assess profitability; if your revenues are growing but profits are stagnant, it might indicate rising costs you need to address. The balance sheet, on the other hand, helps you evaluate financial health by comparing assets to liabilities; a strong balance sheet with more assets than liabilities suggests a robust financial position. Conversely, a high level of liabilities might signal potential cash flow issues. Interpreting the cash flow statement is an important part of business planning, as positive cash flow from operations indicates your business generates enough cash to sustain itself, while negative cash flow might require immediate attention to avoid liquidity problems.

PREPARING FOR TAX SEASON: RECORD-KEEPING AND DEDUCTIONS

I know I keep harping on the importance of record-keeping here, but there's a reason for that: Accurate record-keeping is the backbone of effective tax preparation for your LLC. Keeping meticulous records throughout the year simplifies the tax filing process and allows you to keep compliance with tax regulations.

The types of records your LLC should keep extend beyond just receipts and invoices, though, as you need to retain comprehensive documentation covering all aspects of your business's financial activity. These documents include income statements, which summarize your revenue and expenses over a specific period, and balance sheets, which provide a snapshot of your assets, liabilities, and equity. Bank statements and credit card records are also essential, as they detail your financial transactions and help verify your income and expenses. But there are also payroll records and employee tax forms, such as W-2s and 1099s, that are necessary for reporting employee compensation. Additionally, keep receipts for business expenses and capital purchases; these documents support your claims for deductions and give you the necessary proof should you are face an audit.

Identifying and maximizing tax deductions can significantly reduce your LLC's tax liability. We already mentioned the home office deduction back in Chapter 5, but that's not the only one at your disposal. Vehicle and travel expenses related to business activities can also be deducted, either based on actual expenses or by using the standard mileage rate. Business meals and entertainment costs are also deductible up to 50% (provided they're directly related to your business), and you can deduct office supplies and equipment such as computers, printers, and software. Keeping detailed records of these expenses allows you to take full advantage of these deductions and reduce your taxable income (Berry-Johnson 2024).

Efficiently organizing and storing tax documents is essential for smooth tax preparation and compliance. Digital storage solutions including cloud-based document management systems such as Google Drive or Dropbox are great because they allow you to store and access your records from anywhere securely. They also keep any relevant information from getting lost by automating the organization process, making it easier for you to retrieve documents when you need them.

Creating a filing system for physical documents is equally important, though, so use labeled folders and a dedicated filing cabinet to keep your records organized. Setting up regular review and organization schedules helps keep your documents up-to-date and easily accessible. Reviewing your records monthly or quarterly also helps you stay on top of your financial situation and prepares you for tax season well in advance.

Accurate record-keeping and understanding deductions and credits are fundamental to managing your LLC's finances and keeping in compliance with tax regulations. These practices simplify tax preparation and enable you to take full advantage of your available tax benefits.

7
GROWTH AND SCALING STRATEGIES

So you've set up your LLC, prepped all your tax info and strategies, and gotten your financials in order—what's the next step? The good news is now it's time to worry about something a little less dry than tax forms: growth and scaling.

There are a bunch of things to learn about here; marketing is a cornerstone of any successful business, while securing venture capital will allow you to expand. There's also plenty to know about hiring new employees, and you always want to be on the lookout for how to penetrate new markets and seek out new products. Let's get to it.

MARKETING YOUR LLC: STRATEGIES FOR GROWTH

A strong marketing strategy is the backbone of business growth, increasing brand awareness and ultimately boosting sales and revenue. It's not a stretch to say building a recognizable brand is essential in today's competitive market, more than it ever has been before. You might think of your brand as a logo or a name, but it's more than that: Ultimately, it represents your business's values, personality, and promise. Engaging with your target audience is thus critically important. By understanding their needs, preferences, and behaviors, you can tailor your marketing efforts to your clients, creating lasting relationships and loyalty. This engagement drives sales and revenue, as a well-executed marketing strategy converts interested prospects into paying customers—and keeps them there.

The rise of the Information Age has significantly altered the parameters of marketing, as there are far, far more avenues for audience engagement than there were half a century ago. Digital marketing has become a powerful tool, encompassing social media, email marketing, and content marketing. Social media platforms like Instagram, TikTok, Facebook, and even Pinterest allow you to connect with a global audience, share your brand's story, and engage with customers in real time (Leslie 2024). Email marketing, meanwhile, is a practical, low-cost method to communicate with prospective, current, and former customers. You can nurture leads and drive repeat business by sending personalized and relevant emails, as long as you're good at it (Kajtaz 2023). Content marketing and SEO (Search Engine Optimization) are also extremely important. Creating valuable and engaging content attracts visitors to your website and establishes your brand as an authority in your industry, while SEO involves optimizing your content with keywords and link strategies to rank higher in search engine results, increasing your visibility to potential customers (Yasar 2024).

While online marketing is now hugely important, it isn't the only way to reach prospective customers. Traditional marketing methods, such as print ads, direct mail, and radio/TV ads, do still hold value though, especially for reaching local audiences. While these methods can be more costly than digital options, they can effectively complement your overall marketing strategy. Networking and word-of-mouth marketing are also powerful tactics you shouldn't overlook. Building relationships with other business owners, attending industry events, and encouraging satisfied customers to refer your business can significantly expand your reach.

Creating a comprehensive marketing plan involves several important steps. You want to set clear marketing objectives right out of the gate using the SMART framework, which stands for "specific, measurable, achievable, relevant, and time-bound." Originally created in 1981 by businessman George T. Doran, the SMART system is designed to take more vague business objectives filled with buzzwords and convert them into actual tangible targets. For example, your objective might be to increase website traffic by 20 percent over the next six months rather than simply "get more website traffic synergistically while we're aligned with the bandwidth to pivot away from our core competencies" (Damon).

Next, define your target audience by focusing on your ideal customers' demographics, interests, and pain points. This knowledge allows you to tailor your marketing messages for their specific needs and choose the proper channels to reach them. You also have to allocate a marketing budget, so determine how much you can spend on marketing activities and move those funds across different channels and tactics. Finally, measure and analyze the effectiveness of your marketing efforts. Use tools like Google Analytics to track website traffic, social media insights to monitor engagement, and sales data to assess your campaigns' return on investment (ROI). Regularly reviewing these metrics helps you refine your strategy and optimize your marketing efforts (Angeles 2024).

Case Study: MUD/WTR's Innovative Marketing Approach

Now let's look at a real-world example of creative marketing in action (this one is actually real!). MUD/WTR, a coffee alternative company, has successfully leveraged marketing to carve out a unique space in the health and wellness industry. Their strategy combines storytelling, education, and bold branding to engage their audience and build a loyal customer base.

MUD/WTR uses extensive content marketing to connect with health-conscious consumers. By creating blog posts, videos, and newsletters, the company educates its audience on the benefits of its product, emphasizing its natural ingredients and caffeine-alternative properties. Their content is informative and relatable, addressing the lifestyle and values of their target audience.

Social media plays a major role in their strategy, as MUD/WTR shares aesthetically pleasing product visuals, customer testimonials, and behind-the-scenes insights into their brand through visual-forward platforms like Instagram and TikTok. They actively engage with their audience by responding to comments and encouraging user-generated content, creating a sense of community around their product.

Collaborations with influencers and thought leaders in the wellness space have further amplified their reach. By partnering with individuals who align with their brand values, MUD/WTR has built credibility and expanded its audience. These collaborations and strategic use of paid advertising and targeted email campaigns have driven significant growth.

MUD/WTR's innovative approach demonstrates how a strong marketing strategy that combines content, community, and partnerships can effectively grow a brand, increase awareness, and drive sales. By applying similar principles, you can position your LLC for long-term success (Fox 2021).

SECURING FINANCING: LOANS, INVESTORS, AND GRANTS

If you're going to grow, you're going to need capital, so securing financing is of paramount importance for any LLC aiming to expand. Additional funding can enable you to invest in new technology or equipment, enhancing efficiency and productivity; a bakery could invest in advanced ovens to increase production capacity, while a tech startup might purchase state-of-the-art servers to handle increased web traffic. Expanding into new markets, in particular, often requires substantial capital, from marketing campaigns to physical storefronts. You also need to worry about the investment of hiring additional staff to support these expansions because the human element matters. Adequate financing allows you to bring in skilled employees who can drive your business forward.

Various financing options are available to LLCs, each with its own advantages and disadvantages. Bank loans and lines of credit are traditional financing methods, offering relatively low interest rates and manageable repayment terms—but securing them often requires a strong credit history and substantial collateral. For example, OnDeck offers loan amounts ranging from $5,000 to $250,000, with same-day funding, making it an attractive option for businesses needing quick capital. However, the high minimum annual revenue requirement might be a barrier for smaller LLCs (Chesanik 2024).

Angel investors and venture capital provide another avenue for financing. Both types of investors provide capital in exchange for equity in your business. While this can significantly boost your financial resources, it often comes with the expectation of rapid growth and a say in business decisions, and giving up even some control can feel grating for any business owner. Government grants and programs are another option, offering funds that do not need to be repaid. However, these grants typically require detailed applications and compliance with specific criteria—and they're extremely competitive for pretty obvious reasons.

Preparing a compelling financing proposal is essential for securing any funding, so get started by crafting a clear and compelling business plan that outlines your business objectives, target market, competitive environment, and strategies for achieving your goals. Highlight financial projections and growth potential; investors and lenders want to see that your business has a viable path to profitability. Include detailed financial documentation like income statements, balance sheets, and cash flow projections to demonstrate your business's financial health and potential. Additionally, showcase the strength and experience of your management team to instill confidence in potential investors. Emphasize their expertise, past successes, and how their skills are pivotal to achieving your business goals. If you don't feel your management team has strength and experience to emphasize, well, that's a different problem you're going to want to resolve.

· · ·

Case Study: Securing Venture Capital for a Tech Startup

Scholly, the groundbreaking scholarship search app founded by Christopher Gray, has completely changed how students access college financial aid. Inspired by his own experience securing over $1.3 million in scholarships, Gray launched Scholly in 2013 alongside co-founders Nick Pirollo and Bryson Alef. They developed a compelling pitch deck that showcased Scholly's unique features, such as its user-friendly interface and scholarship matching algorithm. They also highlighted the app's growing user base, market demand for financial aid tools, and Scholly's potential for social impact. The founders' personal experience with the challenges of securing scholarships was a major part of their presentation, adding authenticity to their vision for the company.

Scholly gained early momentum with a successful pitch on *Shark Tank*, where it secured funding from Daymond John and Lori Greiner. This investment allowed the team to scale their platform, enhance their marketing efforts, and grow their user base. Scholly also garnered significant attention from other major investors afterward, including $100,000 each from AOL founder Steve Case's Rise of the Rest Tour and Philadelphia's Startup PHL Angel Fund, enabling the app to expand its reach and technological capabilities (Field 2024).

In 2023, Scholly reached a pivotal milestone when Sallie Mae, a private student loan company, acquired it. This acquisition marked a new chapter in Scholly's mission to make higher education accessible to all, as Sallie Mae made the app free for users and leveraged its resources to scale Scholly's impact further. The deal has enabled Gray and his team to create wealth, invest in new ventures, and provide greater access to education. Scholly's success demonstrates the power of innovation, strategic funding, and partnerships in driving meaningful change and achieving long-term impact (The Scholarship System 2024).

Securing financing for your LLC involves understanding the various options available, preparing a compelling proposal, and demonstrating your business's potential for growth. Whether through bank loans, venture capital, or grants, the right funding can propel your business to new heights.

SCALING OPERATIONS: HIRING, OUTSOURCING, AND AUTOMATION

As you grow your business, you're not just going to increase your revenue—you're also going to have to increase your costs. Scaling operations is thus extremely important for the growth and sustainability of your LLC. Optimizing operations can significantly improve efficiency, support expansion, and reduce operational costs, and increasing production capacity is a fundamental step. Whether you run a manufacturing business or a service-oriented company, scaling up production or service delivery allows you to meet growing demand without compromising on quality. Enhancing service delivery is equally important, as faster and more reliable services can set you apart from competitors. Achieving this while reducing operational costs is the brass ring, as through streamlined processes and efficient resource management, you can reinvest savings into other areas of your business (such as marketing or research and development).

Effective hiring and talent management are thus key components of scaling your operations. Developing a clear job description is the first step to attracting top talent, and a well-crafted job description outlines the responsibilities, qualifications, and expectations for the role. Conducting effective interviews is next, so prepare questions that assess both the technical skills and cultural fit of applicants. After you've gotten through hiring, implementing employee training programs is essential for onboarding new hires and keeping your team updated with the latest skills and knowledge.

Creating a positive workplace culture, meanwhile, is how you retain skilled employees. A supportive and motivating work environment creates loyalty and reduces turnover. This is less of a hassle for you, but it's also financially a good idea, as it literally costs you money to have to hire and train new employees (Team Jobvite 2024). Former Costco CEO Jim Sinegal was well-known for his efforts to retain employees by creating a workplace that enabled them to thrive—for both moral and financial reasons—resulting in a multi-billion dollar growth in the company (ABC News 2005).

Outsourcing specific tasks that your company either can't do or that are a hassle to accomplish can also free up internal resources and improve operational efficiency. Identify non-core activities that can be outsourced, such as payroll processing, customer support, or IT services; if you delegate these tasks to specialized external partners, it allows you to focus on core business activities that drive growth. Selecting reliable outsourcing partners is important, so research potential partners thoroughly, checking their track record, customer reviews, and service quality. Managing outsourced relationships also requires regular communication and clear agreements on performance expectations. Establish key performance indicators (KPIs) to monitor outsourced tasks and keep them up to your standards.

Implementing automation tools can further enhance productivity and streamline operations. Automating repetitive tasks, such as invoicing and payroll, reduces the burden on your team and minimizes the number of potential errors. Using customer relationship management (CRM) systems can help manage customer interactions, track sales, and improve customer service. CRMs store valuable customer data, allowing you to personalize marketing efforts and build stronger relationships (Deshpande 2023). Leveraging marketing automation platforms can also save you time and effort. These tools automate email campaigns, social media posts, and other marketing activities, keeping up consistent and timely communication with your audience (Go 2024).

Staying updated with technological trends is essential for maintaining a competitive edge, so you should regularly review tech advancements to identify new tools and technologies that can improve your operations. Investing in employee training and development allows your team to utilize these new tools effectively. For example, adopting AI-driven customer service solutions can enhance customer support by providing quick and accurate responses to the more basic inquiries, freeing up your team to handle more complex issues. When implemented successfully, this adoption improves customer satisfaction while increasing efficiency.

It's important not to lean too heavily on AI, though. Some CEOs, like Marc Andreesen of Andreesen-Horowitz, appear to believe AI is ultimately the solution to most if not all, business issues and is an unstoppable wave that won't ever fully crest (Berger 2024). But AI may have already hit a wall for quality due to the Habsburg Problem wherein AI can only be trained on so many human-created datasets (because only so many exist) before it starts training on other AI-created material, causing a downward spiral in how well it works (Dupré 2023). There are theories we may be already hitting the limits of what AI is capable of, so while utilizing AI tools isn't a bad idea in the short term, you don't want your business to be reliant on them in case the market is headed for a crash (Zitron 2024).

Scaling operations involves a complex, layered approach, including effective hiring, strategic outsourcing, and adoption of automation tools. By focusing on these areas, you can improve efficiency, support business growth, and maintain a competitive edge in your industry.

EXPANDING YOUR LLC: NEW MARKETS AND PRODUCTS

Expanding your LLC into new markets and developing new products can work wonders to drive growth and increase revenue. Diversification is always a good idea, as spreading out your markets and product lines helps mitigate risks by dispersing your business across different areas. If one of your markets faces challenges, others can then compensate, keeping you from losing your shirt. Moreover, entering new markets or launching new products allows you to capitalize on emerging opportunities that might arise from changing consumer behaviors, technological advancements, or gaps in the market. By staying agile and responsive, you can seize these chances to boost your competitive advantage, making your business more resilient and adaptable to industry changes, in addition to increasing profitability.

Conducting thorough market research is extremely important for identifying and evaluating new opportunities. Analyze market trends and consumer behavior with an eye toward patterns in purchasing habits, preferences, and emerging needs. Industry reports, surveys, and social media insights are a good way to gather this data. Assessing market demand and competition is the next step, so determine the size of the market, potential growth rates, and the level of competition you're going to be facing if you dive in. Understanding your position relative to competitors is another good opportunity to deploy the SWOT analysis I talked about all the way back in Chapter 2. Identifying target demographics, meanwhile, is essential for tailoring your approach; you need to understand the age, gender, income level, and interests of your potential customers if you want to appeal to them. Finally, conduct feasibility studies to evaluate the practicality of entering a new market or launching a new product; factors such as cost, resources required, potential return on investment, and alignment with your business goals all matter here. Once you have identified a promising market, you need to develop a market entry strategy that outlines your approach to the new market, including your goals, timelines, and key activities.

Establishing local partnerships can provide invaluable support if you're getting into a new geographic area, so try to partner where possible with local businesses, distributors, or influencers who can help you work through the market and reach your target audience effectively. Adapt your marketing and sales approaches to fit the new market by tailoring your messaging, branding, and promotional tactics to click with local customers. You're also going to need to understand potential regulatory and cultural issues for compliance and acceptance. Really try to grasp the new market's legal requirements, business practices, and cultural nuances to avoid potential pitfalls and build trust with local customers.

Developing and launching new products involves several steps. Ideation and concept development are up first; brainstorm ideas that align with your market research findings and customer needs. Once you have a viable concept, move on to testing, so create a prototype of your product and conduct experiments to gather feedback and identify any improvements it needs. Pricing and positioning strategies, meanwhile, are the key to market acceptance. Determine a pricing strategy that reflects the value of your product and is competitive within the market, then position your product to highlight its unique benefits and differentiators. The final step is launch planning and execution. Develop a detailed launch plan that includes timelines, marketing campaigns, and distribution strategies, then execute that plan with precision, monitor the results, and be ready to make adjustments as needed.

Case Study: Successful Market and Product Expansions

Apple, a global tech giant, is a prime example of a company that has mastered market and product expansion. One of their most notable successes was their entry into the smartphone market with the iPhone in 2007. At the time, the market was dominated by companies like BlackBerry and Nokia, but Apple identified an opportunity to revolutionize mobile technology with a device that combined a phone, music player, and internet browser. By leveraging its strong brand, exceptional design, and user-friendly interface, Apple created a product that ultimately took over the worldwide cell phone market.

Apple's market expansion strategy was equally meticulous. The company adapted its various marketing campaigns to cater to international markets and align with different regions' cultural nuances and customer preferences. In Europe, for example, they emphasized local partnerships with mobile carriers to guarantee wide distribution. They also focused on creating an ecosystem with complementary products like the app store, which drove further adoption of the iPhone by providing a seamless user experience. Today, the app store is so powerful that when an app is removed from it (a process known as "delisting"), it effectively kills the app entirely (Harris 2022). You may have heard, for example, about the "ban" of TikTok in the United States—only it isn't actually a ban per se, but an order for companies like Apple and Google to delist the app from their stores (Vanian and Mangan 2024).

On the product expansion front, Apple extended its product line by eventually introducing variations of the iPhone, such as the iPhone SE, which catered to budget-conscious consumers while maintaining the brand's premium reputation. Additionally, they launched complementary products like the Apple Watch and AirPods in a bid to enhance the ecosystem and increase customer loyalty. While the former was a bust (Chen 2015), the latter has been a massive success, raking in billions of dollars since they hit the market (White 2020). Hitting on even 50% of their new products allowed Apple to turn huge profits, as the AirPods expansion ultimately succeeded at diversifying their revenue streams and strengthened their market presence.

Apple's approach demonstrates the importance of innovation, strategic localization, and ecosystem building in achieving successful market and product expansions. By understanding customer needs and executing its efforts with precision, the company has consistently stayed ahead of competitors, driving sustained growth and global influence (Coulstring 2024).

Hopefully, it's clear by now that expanding into new markets and developing new products can profoundly impact your LLC's growth and success. By conducting thorough market research, crafting effective strategies, and executing detailed plans, you can capitalize on new opportunities, enhance your competitive edge, and drive significant revenue growth. As you continue to grow and scale your business, these strategies will be instrumental in guaranteeing your long-term success.

8

RISK MANAGEMENT AND LIABILITY PROTECTION

No business venture exists without its risks; everyone faces them, from financial setbacks to operational challenges. You can never fully eliminate risk, but identifying and managing these perils is how you safeguard your LLC and set yourself up for long-term success. By evaluating potential threats ahead of time and implementing effective strategies to prepare for them, you can protect your business and build a foundation for professional resilience.

Understanding the different types of risks your LLC may face is essential for developing a resilient business. By identifying these risks early, you can get ahead of them to mitigate their impact. Addressing risks head-on also builds trust for your LLC among investors, clients, and employees, as it demonstrates that your business can handle challenges effectively.

TYPES OF RISK

Financial risk encompasses a range of challenges that can threaten your LLC's financial stability—market fluctuations, credit issues, liquidity constraints, and even just broader economic trends. Recognizing and addressing these risks is essential to maintaining your business's resilience and preparing for unforeseen challenges.

Compliance Risk

We've covered this one in significant detail already. Compliance risk is basically the threat to your business from failing to comply with laws or regulations. It's both the most catastrophic risk and the easiest to predict, so there's no need to spend further time on it.

Market Risk

Market risk involves external factors that can impact your business's revenue, such as changes in consumer demand, economic downturns, or industry shifts. A sudden dip in the market for your products or services might reduce sales and profitability, causing your sales to go into a downward spiral. Monitoring market trends and diversifying your revenue streams are the best ways of minimizing this risk.

Operational Risk

Operational risks stem from internal processes, systems, or external events that disrupt daily operations—things like equipment failures, supply chain disruptions, or staffing shortages. When a manufacturing business faces delays because a supplier fails to deliver materials on time, that's an operational risk. Establishing efficient processes and diversifying suppliers can help reduce these risks.

Reputational Risk

Reputational risk arises from events that damage your business's public image or credibility. Negative reviews, public relations crises, or legal issues can erode customer trust and hurt your brand. A single misstep on social media can now have widespread consequences, so the best way to handle this type of risk is to proactively manage customer relationships and address complaints to protect your reputation (Kenton 2024c).

Credit Risk

Credit risk arises when clients or partners fail to meet their financial obligations, such as late payments or defaults. We talked a lot about what happens when you miss a payment, but this is the flip side when other people miss a payment to you. Missing payments can disrupt your cash flow and strain your ability to cover operational expenses. To mitigate credit risk, implement clear payment terms, conduct credit checks on clients before your transactions with them, and require deposits or advance payments for high-value transactions (The Investopedia Team 2024).

Liquidity Risk

Liquidity risk occurs when your business lacks the cash or readily accessible assets needed to meet short-term obligations like payroll, rent, or supplier payments. Even profitable businesses can face liquidity issues if cash inflows don't match outflows. Maintaining a cash reserve, securing a line of credit, and closely managing accounts receivable can help you stay liquid and avoid financial strain (Kenton 2024d).

. . .

Inflation Risk

Inflation risk reflects the rising costs of goods, labor, or services, which can erode your profit margins. Fluctuating currency values can affect the cost of imports, exports, or financial obligations. Building inflation projections into your pricing strategy and using hedging instruments for currency exchanges can mitigate these risks (Halton 2022).

By identifying and understanding these risk types, you can assess their potential impact and prioritize them for mitigation. Each of these risks requires different tailored strategies—but don't worry, I've got you covered.

RISK ASSESSMENT

Risks in a business do not exist in isolation; they are interconnected, forming a web where the impact of one risk can ripple through others. A financial risk like a sudden liquidity shortage can quickly lead to operational challenges like delays in vendor payments or employee dissatisfaction. Similarly, reputational damage, perhaps caused by that same disgruntled employee, can decrease sales, circling back around and further exacerbating financial risks. This interconnected nature of risks highlights the importance of assessing and managing them swiftly and effectively.

Identifying, assessing, and controlling risks are how you minimize potential disruptions to your LLC. A comprehensive risk assessment begins with cataloging potential risks and understanding their likelihood and potential impact; this process helps prioritize which risks demand immediate attention and resources over the others. Once risks are identified, evaluate how they interrelate. For example, how could a supply chain issue (operational risk) lead to customer dissatisfaction (reputational risk)?

A risk management plan, meanwhile, serves as a blueprint for identifying vulnerabilities, implementing safeguards, and establishing contingency measures. This proactive approach serves to both reduce the likelihood of severe disruptions and reassure stakeholders that your LLC is prepared to face challenges effectively.

RISK MANAGEMENT TECHNIQUES

Managing risk effectively involves applying strategies that address the likelihood and impact of potential threats. Your approach needs to be tailored to the nature of the risk while maintaining flexibility to adapt as circumstances change. Though the specifics change, the overarching rule remains the same, as three primary techniques—risk avoidance, risk reduction, and risk transfer—form the foundation of a solid risk management framework.

Risk Avoidance

Risk avoidance focuses on eliminating activities or decisions that pose significant threats to your LLC. If entering a high-risk market could jeopardize your financial stability, it may be better to pursue safer opportunities, especially when starting out. Risk avoidance thus outright sidesteps potential risk issues, effectively eliminating them altogether. While avoidance is not always feasible, it can be a prudent strategy for risks with severe potential consequences that outweigh the benefits.

Risk Reduction

Risk reduction, meanwhile, involves implementing measures to minimize the likelihood or impact of a risk. Investing in employee training can reduce operational errors, while maintaining strong cybersecurity protocols lowers the risk of data breaches. Regularly evaluating your processes and systems allows you to identify areas for improvement, strengthening your LLC's resilience against various risks. Risk reduction's value comes into play when you're dealing with a behavior that carries risk that can't be avoided; just existing on the internet in the modern age carries with it significant risks, for instance.

Risk Transfer

Risk transfer shifts the financial burden of a risk to another party, typically through insurance or contractual agreements. Purchasing general liability insurance protects your LLC from costly legal claims, which would count as a type of risk transfer. This strategy shifts potential losses for your business to a third party. In terms of risk vs. reward, this might be the one that protects you the most.

By leveraging these techniques, you can create a balanced risk management approach tailored to your LLC's specific needs. A proactive mindset and clear strategies position your business to deal with challenges so you don't have to worry about pure chaos when things go wrong.

TYPES OF INSURANCE

As I just alluded to, insurance is a cornerstone of any effective risk management strategy. It provides a safety net for your LLC, transferring the financial burden of unexpected events to an insurer. With the right coverage, your business can recover quickly from disruptions and maintain stability. Here are some key types of insurance every LLC should think about:

General Liability Insurance

General liability insurance protects your LLC from claims related to bodily injury, property damage, or advertising harm. If a customer slips and falls at your premises, general liability insurance would cover their medical and your legal expenses. This is one of the most common types of insurance for businesses (Ancheta 2024).

Professional Liability Insurance

Also known as errors and omissions (E&O) insurance, professional liability coverage is essential for service-based businesses. It protects against claims of negligence, mistakes, or failure to deliver promised results. If a consultant provides advice that results in a client's financial loss, professional liability insurance can step in to cover legal fees and damages (Kagan 2024b).

Property Insurance

Property insurance works very similarly to how it does in non-business contests, safeguarding your physical assets, including buildings, equipment, and inventory. Whether damage results from fire, theft, or natural disasters, this coverage helps means your LLC can repair or replace essential assets and continue operating (Twin 2024).

Business Interruption Insurance

Business interruption insurance compensates for lost income and ongoing expenses if your operations are disrupted due to unforeseen events, such as a fire or natural disaster. This policy helps bridge the financial gap during recovery, ensuring your LLC can stay afloat while resuming normal operations (Kagan 2024c).

Selecting and Reviewing Coverage

Choosing the right insurance begins with assessing your business's unique risks. Think about your industry, operations, and assets—what are the risks you face, and which policies offer the most protection? Even after you've gotten your insurance set up, you should still regularly review your coverage to keep it in line with your LLC's needs, then adjust your policies to meet new challenges as your business grows or diversifies.

Whichever type or types you go for, insurance is just generally a good idea for businesses. By investing in comprehensive insurance coverage, your LLC gains the resilience needed to face unexpected events confidently. Insurance protects your business financially, sure, but it also builds trust with stakeholders, demonstrating your commitment to managing risks responsibly.

APPLYING RISK MANAGEMENT TO BUSINESS GROWTH

Risk management doesn't stop at protecting your LLC from threats; it also plays an important role in helping sustainable growth along. By proactively addressing risks, you create a stable foundation that allows your business to scale confidently and strategically with the chance for a disaster kept to a minimum. Growth often involves taking calculated risks—hence why risk avoidance isn't possible all the time—and a strong risk management framework keeps your decisions around these risks informed and measured.

. . .

Reinvesting Profits

One way to fuel growth while managing risk is by reinvesting your profits. Utilize your business's earnings to expand operations, develop new products, or improve infrastructure in order to avoid the pitfalls of taking on excessive debt. This approach minimizes the financial risks you can control while positioning your LLC for long-term success.

External Investment and Financing

While it does come with the potential partial loss of control outlined in Chapter 3, securing external investment is also a good way to manage risk. When you need to access external financing such as loans or investments, meanwhile, a risk management plan will reassure you you're prepared to meet your financial obligations. Securing funding involves assessing repayment capabilities, evaluating investor expectations, and understanding market risks. This preparation protects your LLC from overextending financially and keeps you in good with external capital, supporting rather than endangering your business goals.

Mergers and Acquisitions

Expanding through mergers or acquisitions is often a high-risk, high-reward strategy. When it works, it makes boatloads of money—but it can also come with pitfalls like cultural integration challenges, unforeseen liabilities, and operational disruptions. A comprehensive risk assessment process helps identify potential pitfalls before finalizing deals. This proactive approach makes sure growth opportunities align with your LLC's long-term vision and risk tolerance.

. . .

Risk-Managed Growth in Practice

Applying risk management principles to growth strategies requires integrating them into your business decision-making processes. If you're about to expand, take the time to evaluate how the expansion could impact your financial stability, operations, and reputation. Use your risk assessment tools to identify potential challenges and develop contingency plans that address these risks effectively.

Preserving Liability Protection: Avoiding Piercing the Corporate Veil

As you manage risks and pursue growth opportunities, it's vital to protect the liability shield your LLC provides. Piercing the corporate veil occurs when courts find that the LLC is not being treated as a separate entity, potentially exposing members' personal assets to business liabilities. To prevent this, maintain strict separation between personal and business finances by using dedicated bank accounts and financial records. Comply with all legal and regulatory requirements, such as filing annual reports and keeping operating agreements current. Avoid commingling LLC funds with personal expenses and document major business decisions thoroughly. By following these practices, you can ensure your LLC remains a distinct legal entity, safeguarding your personal assets as your business grows.

In order to keep your LLC resilient and adaptable even in the face of uncertainty, utilize risk management for your growth initiatives. Doing so effectively enables you to seize opportunities with confidence while safeguarding the stability and integrity of your business. Risk management is about protection and preparation. By mastering these strategies, your LLC becomes equipped to face uncertainties while you position it for a seamless transition to whatever comes next.

ACTION STEPS

Designing a risk management plan is essential for protecting your LLC and its long-term success. This step-by-step guide will help you create a customized plan that identifies risks, assesses their impact, and outlines strategies for mitigation. By the end, you'll have a comprehensive framework to manage uncertainties effectively and position your LLC for resilience and growth.

Step 1: Identify Your Industry Sector

Define the scope of your LLC's operations. What industry are you in, and what services or products do you provide? Each industry is going to have specific risks associated with it, and pinpointing them is how you get started.

Step 2: Categorize Potential Risks

List potential risks in key categories: financial, operational, reputational, and external. Include risks such as cash flow challenges, supply chain disruptions, or customer dissatisfaction. Tack on as many as you can think of, including all the ones outlined earlier in this chapter.

Step 3: Evaluate Those Risks

Assess the likelihood and impact of each risk using a simple scale (e.g., low, medium, high). Prioritize risks that are both likely to occur and have a high impact on your LLC. It seems obvious to say, but bigger problems are more immediate than smaller ones!

Step 4: Develop Strategies to Mitigate Risk

For each high-priority risk, outline a specific strategy to mitigate or control it. Use techniques such as risk avoidance, reduction, or transfer. You can move on to the medium and low risks after this, but you want to iron out all the high risks first.

Step 5: Determine Insurance Coverage You Need

Review the types of insurance needed for your LLC—general liability, property, business interruption, or whichever else. Make sure the specific policies you pursue can actually help deal with the risks you already identified.

Step 6: Plan for Future Growth

Incorporate risk management into your growth strategy. Think about how reinvestment of profits, external financing, or partnerships could proactively introduce and address new risks, and plan to pursue whichever are helpful for you.

Step 7: Review and Refine Your Plan

A risk management plan is a living document. Set a schedule to review and update it regularly, incorporating new risks and adjusting strategies as things change. Don't let your risk management plan become stagnant, or you won't be prepared for risks as they arise.

9
OPERATIONAL EXCELLENCE

We've talked a lot about how to deal with problems that might pop up in the course of running an LLC, but what about the day-to-day of the business itself? It's not always going to be lurching from crisis to crisis, and thank heaven for that. So, what are the best ways to deal with run-of-the-mill LLC operations?

While it varies from industry to industry, there are some commonalities. Managing an LLC generally involves balancing multiple responsibilities, from overseeing operations to pursuing growth opportunities, often leaving little time to focus on long-term goals. Effective time management can solve this problem, however, while also improving productivity and reducing stress.

EFFECTIVE TIME MANAGEMENT FOR LLC OWNERS

"Work smarter, not harder" isn't simply some cliché—it really is an effective business strategy. As an LLC owner, you wear multiple hats—manager, marketer, accountant, and more, depending on your industry. Balancing these roles requires a strategic approach to time management so you can handle these responsibilities well without feeling overwhelmed. Correctly executing this balance reduces stress and prevents burnout, allowing you to maintain a healthy work-life equilibrium. Moreover, good time management enhances your decision-making capabilities over the long term, as you'll have the mental clarity to think strategically rather than reactively.

One of the most effective time management techniques is time-blocking, where you allocate specific blocks of time to different tasks throughout your day. This method helps you dedicate enough time to high-priority tasks without interruptions. You might block out two hours in the morning for client work, an hour for administrative tasks, and another hour for strategic planning. By structuring your day, you can maintain focus and productivity, knowing each task has its allocated time.

Another valuable approach is the Eisenhower Matrix, a prioritization framework that helps you categorize tasks based on their urgency and importance. This matrix divides tasks into four quadrants: urgent and important, important but not urgent, urgent but not important, and neither urgent nor important. By focusing on tasks in the first two quadrants, you can prioritize activities that matter to your business goals and either delegate or outright eliminate tasks that don't matter nearly as much (Nevins 2023). Tools like Trello can assist in organizing these tasks, providing visual boards and lists to track progress and deadlines efficiently (He. Johnson 2017).

Setting and achieving daily goals is another important aspect of time management., as breaking down larger projects into smaller, manageable tasks makes them less daunting and more achievable. The SMART criteria we talked about in Chapter 7 becomes useful again here; instead of setting a vague goal like "improve marketing," you could set a SMART goal such as "increase social media engagement by 20 percent over the next three months by posting daily and interacting with followers." Reviewing and adjusting these goals throughout the day keeps you on track and able to adapt to any changes or challenges that come up (Damon n.d.).

Delegating tasks, meanwhile, is an essential skill for LLC owners. Trying to do everything yourself will inevitably lead to overall inefficiency at best and full burnout at worst. Identify tasks you can delegate to others, such as administrative work, bookkeeping, or social media management. Choose team members with the right skills and provide them with clear instructions and support. Delegating effectively frees up your time for more strategic activities, empowers your team, and creates a better, more collaborative work environment. When you do it right, there really isn't a downside.

BUILDING A STRONG TEAM: RECRUITING AND RETAINING TALENT

The importance of delegating brings me to my next topic: building your team. A strong team is the backbone of any successful LLC, as the right team can drive business growth, enhance problem-solving capabilities, and improve customer service. Skilled and motivated employees bring fresh ideas and innovative solutions, helping your business stay competitive and address challenges more effectively. A dedicated team also has the capacity to really enhance customer service, leading to higher satisfaction and retention rates among the people who allow your business to keep existing. And as we talked about already, when customers feel valued and well-served, they are more likely to return and recommend your business to others. Finally, having a strong team supports business scalability and expansion; as your business grows, you'll need reliable and competent employees to handle increased workloads and responsibilities, whether that's helping streamline operations, managing new projects, or maintaining high service standards.

As for how you get to that strong team, the answer is pretty simple: recruitment. Business owners can sometimes view jobs as a gift they deign to patronize the unwashed masses with, but business owners need their workers just as much as they need the person doing the hiring, especially if you want to attract the best and brightest. Start by crafting compelling job descriptions that clearly outline the role's responsibilities, required skills, and benefits so you can attract suitable candidates and set clear expectations from the outset. Leveraging multiple recruitment channels is another effective strategy: Post job openings on popular job boards like Indeed and LinkedIn and use social media platforms to reach a broader audience. Conducting thorough interviews and assessments is essential to connect with the best candidates, so use structured interviews with a mix of behavioral and technical questions to evaluate the candidate's skills and compatibility with your team. Remember to check references and conduct background checks to verify the candidate's qualifications and past performance. Employee referral programs can also be a great idea, especially once you've built a solid team base, as they can speed up the hiring process and make sure those you do bring on board are a good cultural fit.

Onboarding new employees smoothly and effectively, meanwhile, is just as important as hiring them. Develop a comprehensive onboarding program that includes an introduction to your company culture, values, and goals. Once they're ready to get started, provide necessary training and resources to help new hires understand their roles and responsibilities; throwing employees right into the deep end and then blaming them for it when they don't know what to do isn't going to help your business. Assigning mentors or buddies can significantly enhance the onboarding experience, as these experienced employees can offer guidance, answer questions, and help new hires acclimate to their new environment. Setting clear expectations and goals from the beginning also makes sure new hires know what is expected of them and can start contributing to the team effectively.

Retaining top talent is an ongoing effort that requires attention and investment. Offering competitive compensation and benefits is a fundamental aspect of employee retention. Treat your employees well, and they'll treat you well in return. Keep your salary packages in line with industry standards—or above them, if you can afford it and really want to retain your best—and offer attractive benefits such as health insurance, retirement plans, and paid time off. Creating opportunities for professional development matters, too, as employees are more likely to stay with a company that invests in their growth and career advancement. Offer training programs, workshops, and opportunities for promotion. You also need to create a positive and inclusive workplace culture where employees feel valued and respected; this will significantly boost morale and job satisfaction. Recognizing and rewarding employee achievements, meanwhile, is a simple yet powerful way to keep your team motivated. Regularly acknowledge their hard work, whether through bonuses, awards, or public recognition.

UTILIZING TECHNOLOGY TO STREAMLINE OPERATIONS

Embracing technology is pivotal for enhancing operational efficiency in your LLC, as leveraging the right tools can streamline business processes, automate routine tasks, and significantly boost productivity. If you can automate all of your largely mindless repetitive tasks—invoicing, payroll, and data entry—it both frees up your time and that of your employees and reduces the risk of human error. Automating routine tasks allows you to focus on strategic activities that drive growth.

Enhancing communication and collaboration within your team is another benefit of integrating technology. Tools like Slack or Microsoft Teams offer seamless communication channels, enabling real-time messaging and file sharing. They even support video conferencing—which is invaluable for remote teams or when collaborating with clients and partners (Duffy 2021). Improved communication keeps everyone on the same page, reducing misunderstandings and enhancing teamwork. Furthermore, project management software such as GanttPro or Teamwork allows you to assign tasks, set deadlines, and monitor progress, keeping projects on track and team members accountable (Duffy and Moore 2024).

Data management and analysis are other areas in which technology can make a significant impact. CRM systems like Salesforce or Insightly can organize and analyze customer data, helping you understand customer behavior and preferences. This data-driven approach enables you to tailor your marketing strategies and improve customer satisfaction (McAllister 2024). Tools like Google Analytics also offer insights into website traffic and user behavior, allowing you to optimize your online presence (Herrity 2024). Effective data management allows you to make informed decisions based on accurate and real-time information.

Selecting the right technology tools for your LLC involves a thoughtful assessment of your business requirements. What are the specific needs of your business? Are you struggling with project management, customer relationship management, or accounting? Once you have a clear understanding of your needs, research and compare software options that address these pain points. Look for tools that offer the features you need without unnecessary complexity; simpler is better here. The scalability of the software matters, too; choose solutions that can grow with your business and integrate seamlessly with other tools you already use.

Implementing new technology requires careful planning and management. A clear implementation plan that includes timelines, milestones, and responsible team members is a good start. Communicate the benefits of the new technology to your team to gain their buy-in. As with new hires, training matters, so make sure all users receive comprehensive guidelines on the latest tools, whether through workshops, online tutorials, or one-on-one sessions. Regularly monitor the effectiveness of the technology solutions, address any technical issues promptly, and be open to feedback from your team. Continuous evaluation and adjustments will guarantee the technology effectively meets your business needs.

CUSTOMER RELATIONSHIP MANAGEMENT: BEST PRACTICES

Of course, while taking care of your employees is important, it's just as vital to make sure your customers feel their needs are being met. Positive relationships enhance customer loyalty, making clients more likely to return and continue doing business with you. This loyalty translates into increased customer lifetime value, where they spend more over the duration of their relationship with your business. Satisfied customers are also more likely to generate positive word-of-mouth and referrals, bringing new clients to your door without any marketing cost. These elements collectively drive business success by creating a stable and expanding customer base.

Providing exceptional customer service is a critical component of CRM. This means being responsive to customer inquiries, resolving issues promptly, and going above and beyond to exceed their expectations. Excellent service encourages trust and satisfaction, keeping customers loyal and recommending your business to others. Collecting and acting on customer feedback is equally important; regularly solicit how your customers are feeling through surveys, social media, or direct communication to understand your areas for improvement. Implementing changes based on this input shows you value their opinions and are committed to enhancing their experience.

Strong customer relationships are the lifeblood of the success of any customer-facing LLC. By leveraging CRM tools and strategies, you can enhance customer loyalty, increase lifetime value, and generate positive referrals, driving business growth and success. Connecting these elements to the bigger picture, remember that strong relationships lead to loyal customers who return and bring new clients through referrals. This cycle of loyalty and growth is essential for sustaining and expanding your LLC.

10

EXIT STRATEGIES AND SUCCESSION PLANNING

So you've succeeded at all the previous chapters, and now you're running a thriving LLC that you've built from the ground up. You've put in years of hard work, late nights, and countless sacrifices. Finally, the time has come to think about the future—both your future and that of your business. What if you want to get out of the game?

Planning your exit strategy is important not just for your personal financial security but for encouraging the continued success of your company. Without a well-defined exit strategy, you risk leaving your business in disarray, potentially losing the value you've worked so hard to create.

PLANNING YOUR EXIT STRATEGY: OPTIONS AND CONSIDERATIONS

Having a clear and well-defined exit strategy is essential for several reasons:

1. It helps create a smooth transition, which is important for maintaining business operations and relationships with clients, employees, and partners. A seamless handover minimizes disruptions and keeps the business running efficiently.
2. A well-thought-out exit strategy maximizes the value of your business itself. By planning ahead, you can make the necessary adjustments to increase your business's attractiveness to potential buyers or successors, earning you more money on your way out the door.
3. Planning your exit reduces uncertainty and stress. When you don't have to think about how to leave the company in the immediate moment, it allows you to feel confident knowing you have a surefire plan in place.

Several exit strategy options are available to LLC owners, each with its own advantages and challenges. One standard option is selling the business to a third party—generally an outright sale where the buyer takes full control of the business, including its assets and liabilities. Selling to a third party often provides the highest immediate financial return, especially if your business has a strong market presence and profitability.

Another option is selling to business partners or employees. This internal sale can be smoother since the buyers are already familiar with the business operations and culture. There aren't likely to be any internal issues if you go this route, especially since it helps maintain continuity for clients and employees. The major downside here is you're not likely to get as much immediate capital for your investment.

There's also the most gentle option: a gradual exit through phased retirement, which allows you to slowly reduce your involvement in the business over time. This approach provides a gentle transition, giving you time to mentor your successor and keeping the business as stable as humanly possible.

When choosing an exit strategy, you need to think about several different factors. First, evaluate the current business valuation and market conditions; understanding the worth of your business and the market demand will help you determine the best time and method for your exit. Personal financial goals and retirement plans also play a pretty important role. How the exit will impact your financial security? Does your exit strategy match your long-term objectives?

Additionally, think about the impact on your employees and customers. Protecting their interests can help maintain the business's reputation and operational stability. Lastly, assess the timing and readiness of your business. A rushed exit can lead to a lower sale price or operational challenges, so make sure your business is in a strong position before proceeding.

Case Study: Employee Buyout and Transition in a Family-Owned Auto Repair Shop

Near me is a local auto repair shop that has been a trusted service provider in my community for decades. A family initially owned the shop, and my own family had been customers for many years. Over time, we got to know the manager quite well; he had started as a mechanic and worked his way up to become the shop's manager. He had a great rapport with the owner and was deeply invested in the success of the business.

One day, the manager shared the exciting news that he had purchased the shop from the previous owner, officially becoming the new owner. The transition from manager to owner was smooth, with the manager maintaining strong relationships with both the employees and long-time customers. His intimate knowledge of the business and his personal ties to the community made him the ideal person to carry the shop forward.

This buyout provided the original owner with a comfortable retirement and kept the business thriving under leadership that was already deeply familiar with its operations and values. The new owner kept the business's core principles intact, retaining the experienced staff and maintaining the high level of service customers had come to expect. As a result, the shop continued to build on its reputation for trustworthiness, and customers, like my family, remained loyal to the business for years to come.

Planning your exit strategy is ultimately about preserving the legacy and success of what you've built. You don't just want to abandon your hard-earned creation to the whims of fate, so you really want to carefully consider your options and planning to maximize your business's value and guarantee a smooth transition. Whether you choose to sell to a third party, sell to your own employees, or implement a phased retirement, having a well-thought-out plan will make the process smoother and more successful.

VALUING YOUR LLC: METHODS AND FACTORS

Of course, you have to know what your business is worth to get the most out of selling it. Accurately valuing your LLC is extremely important when it comes to setting the right price and negotiating a sale because knowing the fair market value and sticking to your guns during negotiations guarantees you receive the true worth of your business. Buyers who see a well-justified valuation are more likely to trust the figures and proceed with the transaction. A precise valuation also helps with securing loans and attracting investors—both of which hinge on the perceived value of your business.

There are several common methods for valuing an LLC, each with its unique approach. One popular route is asset-based valuation, which calculates the net asset value of your business by subtracting its total liabilities from its total assets. This is a particularly good option for businesses with significant tangible assets. Another method is income-based valuation, which focuses on the company's ability to generate future earnings. This type of valuation involves using metrics like Earnings Before Interest, Taxes, Depreciation, and Amortization (EBITDA) and applying a multiplier based on specific industry standards (Hayes 2024d). Market-based valuation, on the other hand, compares your LLC to similar businesses that have recently been sold. This route makes use of market comparables to estimate a fair market value, providing a realistic snapshot of what buyers might be willing to pay.

There are a bunch of different factors that can influence the value of an LLC, and the easiest to understand is probably financial performance and profitability. Buyers scrutinize your revenue streams, profit margins, and overall financial health, and a profitable, financially stable business commands a higher valuation. Simple enough, really.

Market position and competitive advantage also play significant roles, as a company with a strong brand, unique products, or a dominant market position is more attractive to buyers. Customer base and revenue stability are equally important because a diverse, loyal customer base with recurring revenue streams indicates reliability and reduces perceived risk. Finally, growth potential and scalability can substantially boost your LLC's value; buyers are willing to pay a premium for businesses with clear paths to expansion and the ability to scale operations efficiently.

So, how do you increase the sale value of your LLC? Improving financial performance and efficiency is the most obvious route. Streamline operations, reduce unnecessary expenses, and optimize profit margins to present a more substantial financial picture. Strengthening customer relationships and loyalty can also enhance value, so implement customer retention strategies based on high satisfaction levels. Developing a clear, forward-looking business plan that outlines growth opportunities, market expansion, and strategic initiatives can also significantly increase your business's attractiveness. Investing in technology and innovation is equally important; adopting the latest technologies and innovative practices improves operational efficiency and positions your business as forward-thinking and competitive.

A few terms here can help you focus on improving key performance indicators (KPIs). These include things like customer acquisition cost (CAC) and customer lifetime value (CLV). CAC is an approximation of what it would cost to acquire new customers relative to what you pay for them in things like your marketing budget and how much it costs to pay the employees doing the acquiring (Kotlyar). CLV, meanwhile, is a metric that helps you determine how much you can earn from an average customer over the lifetime of their business (Caldwell 2022). Lowering CAC through efficient marketing strategies while increasing CLV by enhancing customer experience can significantly boost profitability. I know these are a bunch of letters and might feel like alphabet soup right now, but they're important to remember.

You should also explore opportunities to diversify your product or service offerings since a broader portfolio can attract a wider customer base and reduce dependency on a single revenue stream. Maintaining transparent and accurate financial records is important, too; potential buyers are likely to conduct thorough due diligence, and clean, well-organized books can expedite the process and build trust. After all, you don't want to torpedo the sale when buyers find out something unpleasant you tried to hide from them.

SELLING YOUR LLC: PROCESS AND TIPS

The process of selling your LLC involves several steps, and each of them is important for a smooth and profitable transition. Preparing the business for sale is the first and most important step. Conduct a thorough financial audit to identify and rectify any discrepancies in your financial statements; this will give potential buyers a clear and accurate picture of your business's financial health and ultimately serve to make a purchase more attractive. Streamlining operations and reducing costs can also enhance your business's appeal, as efficient operations and lower costs indicate a well-managed, profitable business, which is always more attractive to buyers. Additionally, focus on enhancing your company's public image and brand to minimize reputational risk and highlight how your image speaks for you.

Once your business is prepared for sale, the next step is identifying potential buyers. Sometimes, they'll come to you, but you can find them yourself, too, if you put in the legwork. This can be done through various channels, including business brokers, industry contacts, and networking events. Business brokers can be particularly useful as they can access a broad network of potentials and help match your business with the right buyer.

Effectively marketing the business is also essential to securing a good price. Create a compelling sales prospectus highlighting your business's strengths, financial performance, and growth potential. To reach a wide audience, use multiple marketing channels, including online business-for-sale platforms, industry publications, and social media. Empire Flippers could be a phenomenal platform to market and sell your business to potential buyers if you own an online business. They also have a free valuation tool on their website to estimate how much you can sell your business (Ghezelbash 2024).

Negotiating the sale agreement is its own sort of beast involving discussions around the sale price, payment terms, and any conditions or contingencies. It's essential to approach these negotiations with a clear understanding of your business's value and your desired outcomes. Be prepared to provide detailed information and answer questions from potential buyers; a well-prepared sales agreement outlining all terms and conditions can help facilitate a smooth negotiation process. When you're finally ready to close the deal, you'll finalize the sale agreement, transfer ownership, and meet all legal and financial obligations. This may include updating the operating agreement, notifying the state of the ownership change, and handling any remaining financial transactions.

Case Study: The $1.7 Million Amazon FBA Business Sale

There are more examples of incredible LLC sales than you might realize. In 2017, an Amazon FBA entrepreneur made headlines by selling their thriving e-commerce business for $1.7 million on the Empire Flippers marketplace. Even though this business had been built over just a few years, the sellers were able to leverage Amazon's vast organic traffic and high conversion rates to generate steady monthly profits of $40,000–with minimal operational costs, no less. Despite its success, the owner decided to sell. The risks of relying solely on Amazon's platform were just too great, not to mention the seller's desire to diversify their income streams by investing in other ventures.

The sale process was meticulously planned, and there was a comprehensive vetting of the business to highlight its revenue, profit margins, and scalability. Empire Flippers connected the seller with several interested buyers–including investment groups eager to acquire such a valuable digital asset. After months of negotiations, a deal was finalized for $850,000 upfront followed by structured payouts tied to revenue milestones. This arrangement mitigated risks for the buyer while ensuring the seller retained financial security throughout the transition.

The migration process involved transferring ownership of the Seller Central account and ensuring the buyer had the tools and knowledge to manage inventory and maintain customer satisfaction. The structured deal allowed the buyer to upscale the business, while the seller used the proceeds to diversify into those new ventures they were so interested in. Ultimately, this sale illustrates how strategic planning, diligent preparation, and leveraging expert advisors can lead to a successful exit. With skill, preparation, and timing, you too could turn a few years of hard work into a multimillion dollar payday (Elfrink 2020).

SUCCESSION PLANNING: PASSING YOUR LLC TO THE NEXT GENERATION

Succession planning for family-owned businesses is an important aspect that keeps the continuity and legacy of your hard work going through the generations that succeed you. Handing over the reins directly to family allows you to preserve the values and culture that have been the bedrock of your business. Planning for those who come after you guarantees a smooth and seamless transition, minimizing disruptions that could affect operations. It also serves to preserve your family legacy, keeping the business thriving under the stewardship of the next generation. It's not all flowers and sunshine, though; without a clear succession plan, you might run afoul of family conflicts and legal disputes, potentially jeopardizing both personal relationships and the business itself.

Creating a comprehensive succession plan involves several steps. Identifying potential successors within the family or the business is a pretty clear starting point. You'll want to assess the skills, interests, and commitment levels of family members or key employees, which might involve several people if there's not one clear successor. Not everyone will be suited for leadership roles, so it's important to evaluate their readiness and willingness to take on the significant responsibility of inheriting the business. Once you've identified your potential successor or successors, develop a training and development plan to prepare them for their future roles. This may include formal education, mentorship programs, and hands-on experience in various aspects of the business. Establishing a timeline for the transition is also essential, as a clear timeline helps manage expectations and provides a structured approach to the handover.

Legal and financial planning plays a significant role in succession planning, too. If you regularly update your operating agreement to reflect changes in management and ownership, you'll be prepared when the time comes. In particular, it should outline the roles and responsibilities of successors, as well as the procedures for transferring ownership. Creating wills and trusts can also provide clarity on the distribution of assets and help avoid potential legal disputes.

Tax planning is another important part of any handover. Understanding the tax implications of transferring ownership can help minimize tax liabilities and keep the transition smooth and easy. One option is to fund the succession through life insurance or buy-sell agreements, which can provide the necessary funds to buy out other family members or business partners, keeping the business financially stable.

Case Study: Succession Planning Through Comprehensive Estate Planning

Let's look at the hypothetical example of Bill, the owner of a beloved restaurant and bar that served as both a livelihood and a family legacy. While Bill's children, Julia and Charles, were actively involved in the business, the lack of a formal legal structure about the future transfer of ownership and associated real estate worried Bill.

To address these challenges, Bill worked with advisors to implement a comprehensive estate planning strategy. First, they formed a multiple-member LLC to structure the business legally, which provided liability protection for family members and created a clear path for transferring ownership to Julia and Charles while maintaining operational continuity.

In addition to the LLC, a realty trust was established to manage and protect the real estate tied to the business. The trust offered a clear framework for transferring ownership, keeping the family's valuable real estate within the family. Bill also created essential estate planning documents, including a will, healthcare proxy, and power of attorney. These tools empowered him to outline his preferences for asset distribution, healthcare decisions, and financial management, providing clarity and reducing potential disputes.

Through these proactive measures, Bill did everything in his power to keep the business a thriving family legacy for generations. His approach highlights the importance of combining a formal business structure with estate planning to address operational and personal succession planning (Segal 2024).

DISSOLVING YOUR LLC: LEGAL AND FINANCIAL STEPS

Dissolving an LLC can be a difficult decision, but sometimes it's also a necessary one. One common reason is financial difficulties; if your business is no longer sustainable due to mounting debts or declining revenue, dissolution might be the best course of action. Or what if you retire without a successor? If no one is able or willing to take over, closing the business can be a practical choice. Strategic shifts or reorganizations also sometimes require dissolving the current entity to form a new structure that better aligns with long-term goals. Lastly, mutual agreement among members can lead to dissolution, especially if your original objectives have been met or circumstances have significantly changed.

The legal process of dissolving an LLC involves several steps to keep in compliance with state laws and protect the interests of all parties involved. The first step is voting on dissolution according to the procedures outlined in the operating agreement, which should include the required approval from members. Once the decision is made, you have to file articles of dissolution with the state where you had the LLC formed. This filing officially notifies the state of your intent to dissolve the business.

You also need to cancel any business licenses and permits associated with your LLC in order to keep you from being liable for regulatory requirements or fees. Additionally, notifying creditors and settling any outstanding debts is another important step. This process involves informing all creditors of the dissolution and making arrangements to pay off any remaining obligations. Don't skip this step; failing to settle debts can lead to legal complications or damage your personal credit.

Financial considerations are important when dissolving an LLC, too. Liquidating business assets by selling inventory, equipment, and other tangible assets is often necessary to pay off debts and distribute the leftover funds to members. Once you have liquidated the assets, the remaining funds should be distributed to members according to the proportions specified in the operating agreement, keeping the process fair and transparent and reducing the potential for disputes.

Finalizing tax obligations is also important since you don't want to deal with the potential legal exposure from failing to deal with your taxes. You have to file a final tax return for the LLC, reporting any income, expenses, and capital gains or losses. You also have to make sure all payroll taxes and sales taxes are settled. The last step is notifying the IRS of the dissolution, and you may need to cancel your EIN.

Always be sure to maintain communication with all stakeholders to keep anything from going wrong. Inform employees, clients, and suppliers about the decision to dissolve the business, and do so clearly since concise communication helps maintain professional relationships and sets the stage for future endeavors. Documenting all steps and decisions made during the dissolution process—things like records of meetings, votes, and financial transactions—is important, too, since proper documentation provides a clear trail, which can be useful if any disputes pop up later (Feldman 2024).

Dissolving your LLC involves careful planning and execution. By understanding the reasons for dissolution, following the legal process, and managing financial issues, you can keep the business's closure as smooth as its operations (or hopefully smoother, if a rocky professional life is the reason you're dissolving it in the first place). You want to minimize stress, protect your personal and financial interests, and allow yourself to move forward confidently should you choose to pursue a different venture, and this is how you do it.

11

INTERNATIONAL ENTREPRENEURS

What about international examples, though? Let's say there's a woman named Maria, an ambitious entrepreneur from Spain, who has decided to expand her online education business into the US market. When she first arrives, she faces a maze of regulations and requirements that seem overwhelming at first. Yet, with careful planning and the right guidance, she successfully establishes her LLC in the US, opening new avenues for growth. For international entrepreneurs like Maria, understanding the specific steps involved in forming an LLC in the US is clearly pretty important.

FORMING AN LLC AS A NON-U.S. RESIDENT: KEY STEPS

Forming an LLC as a non-US resident involves several steps, each of which must be carefully executed to keep in compliance with US laws. The first step is choosing the state in which to form your LLC. States like Delaware, Wyoming, and New Mexico are popular choices due to their business-friendly regulations and tax benefits. Delaware, for instance, is favored by investors for its well-established legal framework, although it comes with higher fees. Wyoming offers the advantage of low costs and no state corporate or personal income tax, while New Mexico is attractive for its low filing costs and the lack of an annual report requirement (Horwitz 2023).

Once you have chosen the state, the next step is filing the articles of organization and obtaining a registered agent. We already covered this in Chapter 3, and the basic requirements are the same for US residents, so we don't need to go into more detail here.

There are differences in documentation, though. The documentation required for non-US residents to form an LLC includes copies of their passports and other identification to verify their identity. Proof of address is also necessary, which can be in the form of utility bills or bank statements. Additionally, if applicable, you must provide information about your visa or residency status.

Managing an LLC remotely as an international entrepreneur requires leveraging technology and strategic planning. One effective strategy is utilizing virtual offices and mail forwarding services—which is invaluable if you're not actually going to be in the country. Virtual offices provide a physical address for your LLC, which can be used for official correspondence and legal documents. Mail forwarding services make sure any important mail received at this address is promptly forwarded to you, regardless of your location. This setup allows you to maintain a professional presence in the US while managing your business from abroad.

Technology plays an important role in facilitating communication and collaboration for remote LLC management. Tools like video conferencing, project management software, and cloud storage enable you to stay connected with your team and manage operations effectively. Platforms such as Zoom, Trello, and Google Drive that offer solutions for virtual meetings, task management, and document sharing. These are useful for everyone, but they're particularly important for international entrepreneurs.

Employing local representatives or managers can also enhance the management of your US-based LLC. Hiring a local manager who understands the US market and regulatory environment can provide valuable on-the-ground insights and keep day-to-day operations running smoothly. This approach allows you to delegate responsibilities while retaining strategic control over your business. Local representatives can handle tasks such as customer service, compliance, and marketing, keeping your LLC competitive and compliant with US regulations (US Citizenship and Immigration Services 2024).

Tax Implications for International LLC Owners

Dealing with the US tax environment as a non-US resident can seem intricate (it's not a fun time for US residents, either). As an international LLC owner, you must meet both federal and state tax obligations. Federally, the US requires you to file an income tax return if your LLC has US-sourced income. If you own a single-member LLC, it is typically classified as a "disregarded entity" for tax purposes, meaning income flows directly to you and is reported on Form 1040NR (Kurt 2022). Multi-member LLCs are treated as partnerships, requiring Form 1065 to report income, deductions, and credits (Simons 2024). Additionally, irrespective of income, foreign-owned LLCs must file Form 5472 (Wallace 2024) alongside a proforma

Form 1120 to disclose reportable transactions with foreign owners or related parties (Internal Revenue Service 2024e).

Tax treaties between the U.S. and other countries can significantly impact your tax liabilities. These treaties aim to prevent double taxation and promote economic cooperation between countries like the UK, Canada, and Germany. These treaties often provide benefits such as reduced withholding tax rates on dividends, interest, and royalties. To claim these treaty benefits, you must complete and submit Form W-8BEN to the IRS, certifying your eligibility. This form helps keep you taxed at the lower treaty rate rather than the standard rate, optimizing your tax obligations (Chen 2024).

Obtaining an Individual Taxpayer Identification Number (ITIN) is essential for international entrepreneurs who need to file US tax returns but are not eligible for a Social Security Number. The application process involves submitting Form W-7 to the IRS, either by mail or through an IRS-authorized Acceptance Agent. You will need to provide supporting documentation, such as a certified copy of your passport, to verify your identity and foreign status. The processing time for receiving an ITIN can vary, typically taking around six to eight weeks. Once obtained, the ITIN will be used on all US tax filings and communications with the IRS (Kagan 2024d).

Withholding taxes is another important consideration for international LLC owners. The US imposes withholding taxes on certain types of income paid to foreign persons, such as dividends, interest, and royalties. The standard withholding tax rate is 30 percent, but this can be reduced or exempted under applicable tax treaties (Langager 2024). To comply with withholding tax requirements, you have to file Form 1042-S to report your income subject to withholding and the amount withheld. This form gives the IRS accurate information about the payments made to foreign persons and the taxes withheld from them. Failure to comply with these requirements can result in significant penalties (Thomson Reuters Tax & Accounting 2024).

Potential exemptions under tax treaties can further reduce your tax burden. For example, many treaties provide exemptions or reduced rates for income derived from certain activities, such as teaching, research, or business profits not attributable to a permanent establishment in the US. There are too many based on too many different countries to list here, so be sure to do research into which treaties might apply to you so you can thoroughly understand the specific provisions of the applicable treaty to see if you qualify. Consulting with a tax professional who specializes in international taxation can help you a lot here.

Understanding the tax implications for international LLC owners involves dealing with a complex web of federal and state requirements, tax treaties, and withholding obligations. By familiarizing yourself with these regulations and seeking professional advice when needed, you can keep compliance and optimize your tax strategy for your US-based LLC.

WORKING THROUGH US BUSINESS REGULATIONS AS AN INTERNATIONAL ENTREPRENEUR

When establishing a foreign-owned LLC in the US, it's important to understand the large number of regulations you're going to have to maneuver through. Federal regulations are the first hurdle, and they encompass a range of laws enforced by agencies like the IRS and the Federal Trade Commission (FTC). The IRS oversees tax compliance, requiring you to file appropriate tax returns and maintain meticulous financial records. The FTC, on the other hand, establishes fair business practices and enforces laws against deceptive advertising and antitrust violations. These federal regulations form the backbone of your compliance obligations, and you'll have to follow them to engage in legal and ethical operations.

Each state has its own set of business laws and regulations, which vary significantly. Some states have stringent annual reporting requirements, while others may have minimal ongoing compliance obligations. There are a lot of these laws and regulations, and since there are fifty states (not including territories like Washington D.C., Puerto Rico, and Guam), you're going to have to do some research to find out which ones apply to you. Fortunately, there's a good place to look for: State government websites often provide comprehensive guides and resources. Additionally, some states require foreign-owned LLCs to register as a "foreign entity" if they conduct business outside their formation state (which isn't the same as being "foreign," technically, as domestic businesses from other states also have to register as foreign entities). This step involves additional paperwork and fees (Schmidt 2024).

Local licensing and permit requirements further complicate the regulatory situation. These requirements depend on the specific location and nature of your business; a restaurant in New York City would need a different set of permits compared to an online consulting firm based in California. Local governments often require businesses to obtain general business licenses, health permits, and zoning permits to operate legally, and failing to secure these licenses can result in fines and legal issues.

Local government websites are the best resource for understanding which specific rules you need to follow. Once you have identified the required licenses, complete the application procedures by filling out forms, providing business details, and paying application fees. Some licenses may require inspections or additional documentation, such as proof of insurance. After submitting your application, it's important to track its progress and follow up if necessary; things can sometimes get lost or delayed in the government shuffle.

Understanding employment laws is another pitfall for international LLC owners, especially when hiring US-based employees. Federal employment laws, such as the Fair Labor Standards Act (FLSA) and the Americans with Disabilities Act (ADA), set the minimum standards for wages, overtime pay, and workplace discrimination. The FLSA mandates minimum wage and overtime pay for eligible employees (Kenton 2023), while the ADA prohibits discrimination based on disability and requires reasonable accommodations (Hayes 2024e). Complying with these laws is mandatory to avoid legal repercussions. To be fair, the US is sometimes regarded as the worst wealthy nation for workers' rights, so it's entirely possible another country's standards will already be significantly higher (Ghilarducci 2023).

State-specific labor regulations, meanwhile, add another layer of complexity. Each state has its own labor laws, which can be more stringent than federal standards. Some states have higher minimum wage rates or additional employee protections; the federal minimum wage is only $7.25, but California's is $16, for example (National Conference of State Legislatures 2024).

Staying compliant with US regulations requires ongoing effort and vigilance. Setting up a compliance calendar is an effective strategy to keep track of important deadlines, such as tax filings, license renewals, and regulatory updates, particularly if you're not used to operating in the US This calendar should be accessible to key team members to make sure everyone is aware of upcoming obligations.

Regularly reviewing and updating business policies matters, too. As laws and regulations change, your business policies should adapt accordingly—and it can be particularly difficult to follow these changes if you're not personally located in the U.S. and paying attention to US news. Conduct periodic reviews of your operating procedures, employee handbooks, and compliance programs so they remain current and effective. Engaging in continuous education on regulatory changes, attending workshops, and participating in industry forums can also keep you informed and prepared for any new compliance challenges.

LEVERAGING US MARKET OPPORTUNITIES: TIPS FOR SUCCESS

Stepping into the US market presents a myriad of opportunities for international businesses. One of the most compelling advantages is access to a large and diverse consumer base, as the United States is the third-largest country in the world by population, home to over 341 million people with varied tastes, preferences, and spending habits (O'Neill 2024). This diversity allows businesses to target multiple market segments, increasing the overall potential for sales and growth. Additionally, the US boasts a generally favorable business environment and robust infrastructure by world standards. With a well-established legal framework, reliable shipping (if not public) transportation networks, and advanced technology, the US provides a conducive setting for businesses to operate efficiently and effectively. The opportunities for innovation and collaboration are also abundant, as the US is a global leader in technology and innovation, making it an ideal place for businesses to develop new products, services, and partnerships (Dyvik 2024).

To successfully enter the US market, you'll need to conduct thorough market research. Start by understanding the competitive environment, identifying important players, and analyzing market trends. Market research helps you gauge demand for your product or service, identify potential gaps, and tailor your offerings to meet local needs. Developing a localized marketing strategy, meanwhile, involves adapting your marketing messages and campaigns to click with US consumers. Think about cultural nuances, language preferences, and local trends when crafting your marketing materials. Building partnerships with US businesses can also significantly enhance your market entry, as collaborating with local companies can provide valuable insights, resources, and networks to help give you a much clearer picture of the market overall.

Cultural adaptation plays a pivotal role in the success of international businesses in the US. Understanding and respecting cultural differences can enhance your interactions with customers, partners, and employees. Dealing with cultural differences in business practices involves familiarizing yourself with US business etiquette, communication styles, and negotiation tactics. For instance, US business culture often values direct communication and promptness relative to some other countries. Adapting your communication styles and marketing messages to match these preferences can improve your business relationships. Building trust and relationships with US stakeholders is essential, as trust is an important component of business success in the US, and building strong relationships requires consistent communication, reliability, and transparency (Mellgren 2023).

Entering the US market offers a wealth of opportunities for international businesses. Accessing a large and diverse consumer base, operating in a favorable business environment, and leveraging opportunities for innovation and collaboration can drive significant growth.

By following the strategies outlined here, international entrepreneurs can capitalize on the vast potential of the US market, achieving growth and establishing a strong presence.

YOUR REVIEW, THEIR INSPIRATION

If you've ever talked to someone else about setting up a business, you'll know that many people are mystified by the whole process. This is your chance to help other entrepreneurs out as they begin their LLC journey, helping them forge a path forward without the mystery.

Simply by sharing your honest opinion of this book and a little about how it's helped you, you'll show new readers where they can find this essential guidance—and you'll inspire them to take the plunge.

Thank you so much for your support. Together, we can help more people to see their dreams come to fruition.

Scan the QR code below:

Or visit:

https://www.amazon.com/review/review-your-purchases/?asin=1967516014

CONCLUSION

Creating your own limited liability company can seem like a daunting task, especially if you're starting with zero experience. My goal here has been to demystify this process for you and to provide you with a comprehensive, step-by-step approach that simplifies the ins and outs of forming, managing, and growing your LLC. I understand the challenges that come with starting a business, and I aim to make this process as accessible and straightforward as possible.

Now, it's your turn to take the first step. Use this book as your practical guide and reference throughout your entrepreneurial experiences. The benefits of forming an LLC are immense, from protecting your personal assets to enjoying significant tax advantages and the flexibility to manage your business as you see fit. Starting now means you're one step closer to achieving your business goals and creating a fulfilling life through your LLC.

Thank you for choosing this book and trusting our collective expertise. I'm honored to support you in this phase of your entrepreneurial life. Remember, you have the tools and knowledge needed to succeed, and I believe in your potential to build a thriving LLC.

I also invite you to share your experiences, ask questions, and provide feedback. Join our online community, where you can connect with me and other entrepreneurs. Your insights and stories are valuable, and they can inspire others during their experiences.

As you close this book, remember that you are empowered and equipped to take on the challenges and opportunities that lie ahead. Your adventure toward creating a successful LLC is just beginning, and with determination and the right guidance, there's no limit to what you can achieve. Embrace the adventure, and know that you have the support and resources to create a prosperous and fulfilling business.

REFERENCES

Abbott, Cole. 2024. "The SMART Framework: How to Set Better Business Goals." *Ninety.io,* September 27. Accessed December 10, 2024. https://www.ninety.io/founders-framework/articles/smart-framework

ABC News. 2005. "Costco CEO Finds Pro-Worker Means Profitability." December 1. Accessed on December 12, 2024. https://abcnews.go.com/2020/Business/story?id=1362779

Ancheta, Andrew. 2024. "What Does Commercial General Liability (CGL) Insurance Cover?" *Investopedia,* July 17. Accessed on December 12, 2024. https://www.investopedia.com/terms/c/commercial-general-liability-cgl.asp

Angeles, Sara. 2024. "How to Use Google Analytics." *Business News Daily*, November 21. Accessed on December 12, 2024. https://www.businessnewsdaily.com/6027-how-to-use-google-analytics.html

Ayoola, Elizabeth. 2024. "5 Self-Employed Retirement Plans to Consider." *NerdWallet,* November 4. Accessed on December 11, 2024. https://www.nerdwallet.com/article/investing/retirement-plans-self-employed

Bank of America. 2024. "Why and How to Keep Your Personal and Business Finances Separate." January 29. Accessed on December 11, 2024. https://business.bankofamerica.com/resources/why-and-how-to-keep-your-personal-and-business-finances-separate.html

Beaulieu, Connor. 2024. "How to Check Business Name Availability: 5 Methods." *Legal Zoom,* November 26. Accessed on December 10, 2024. https://www.legalzoom.com/articles/how-to-find-out-if-a-business-name-is-taken

Berger, Chloe. 2024. "'We're Running Out of Human Knowledge' to Train AI—But Marc Andreessen Believes That Will Create a Hiring Boom." *Fortune,* November 15. Accessed on December 12, 2024. https://fortune.com/2024/11/15/marc-andreessen-ai-replace-jobs-hiring-boom/

Berry-Johnson, Janet. 2024. "17 Big Tax Deductions (Write Offs) for Businesses." *Bench,* June 4. Accessed on December 12, 2024. https://www.bench.co/blog/tax-tips/small-business-tax-deductions

Caldwell, Austin. 2022. "What Is Customer Lifetime Value (CLV) & How to Calculate?" *NetSuite,* July 20. Accessed on December 13, 2024. https://www.netsuite.com/portal/resource/articles/ecommerce/customer-lifetime-value-clv.shtml

REFERENCES

Chafin, Jill A. 2024. "29 Small Business Tax Deductions For Your Business." *Lending Tree*, January 31. Accessed on December 9, 2024. https://www.lendingtree.com/business/home-business-tax-deductions/

Chen, James. 2024. "W-8BEN: When to Use It and Other Types of W-8 Tax Forms." *Investopedia*, July 25. Accessed on December 14, 2024. https://www.investopedia.com/terms/w/w8form.asp

Chen, Brian X. 2015. "Apple's New Job: Selling a Smartwatch to an Uninterested Public." *New York Times*, February 27. Accessed on December 12, 2024. https://www.nytimes.com/2015/03/02/technology/apples-new-job-selling-a-smartwatch-to-an-uninterested-public.html

Chesanik, Carissa. 2024. "OnDeck Business Loan Review." *Lending Tree*, June 18. Accessed on December 12, 2024. https://www.lendingtree.com/business/reviews/ondeck/

Coulstring, Mark. 2024. "IPHONE HISTORY: FROM THE ORIGINAL IPHONE TO IPHONE 16." *SeamGen*, October 1. Accessed on December 12, 2024. https://www.seamgen.com/blog/iphone-history-original-iphone-to-current-iphone

Crawford, Hillary. 2024. "FreshBooks Review 2024." *NerdWallet*, May 13. Accessed on December 11, 2024. https://www.nerdwallet.com/reviews/small-business/freshbooks

d'Viola, Ramona. 2022. "Naming Your LLC: Rules and Requirements for All 50 States." *HelloSkip*, February 17. Accessed on December 9, 2024. https://helloskip.com/blog/naming-your-llc-rules-and-requirements-for-all-50-states

Damon, Chelsea. "Everything You Need to Know About SMART Goals." *AchieveIt*. Accessed on December 12, 2024. https://www.achieveit.com/resources/blog/everything-you-need-to-know-about-smart-goals/

Deshpande, Indrajeet. 2023. "What Is Customer Relationship Management (CRM)? Tools, Types, Strategy, Benefits & Features." *Spiceworks*, August 10. Accessed on December 12, 2024. https://www.spiceworks.com/marketing/crm-marketing/articles/what-is-customer-relationship-management-crm/

Duffy, Jill. 2021. "The Best Business Messaging Apps." *PC Mag*, December 22. Accessed on December 13, 2024. https://www.pcmag.com/picks/the-best-business-messaging-apps

Duffy, Jill and Ben Moore. 2024. "The Best Project Management Software for 2024." *PC Mag*, November 13. Accessed on December 13, 2024. https://www.pcmag.com/picks/the-best-project-management-software

Dupré, Maggie Harrison. 2023. "When AI Is Trained on AI-Generated Data, Strange Things Start to Happen." *Futurism*, August 2. Accessed

REFERENCES

on December 12, 2024. https://futurism.com/ai-trained-ai-generated-data-interview

Dyvik, Einar. 2024. "Technology Leading Countries Worldwide Within Different Industries in 2021." *Statista*, July 4. Accessed on December 14, 2024. https://www.statista.com/statistics/1345283/worldwide-leading-countries-technology-area/

Edwards, John. 2024. "LLC vs. Incorporation: Which Should I Choose?" *Investopedia*, February 21. Accessed on December 9, 2024. https://www.investopedia.com/articles/personal-finance/011216/llc-vs-incorporation-inc-which-should-i-choose.asp

Enright, Mike. 2022. "How to Choose a Registered Agent For Your Business." *Wolters Kluwer*, January 26. Accessed on December 10, 2024. https://www.wolterskluwer.com/en/expert-insights/how-to-choose-a-registered-agent-for-your-business

Evans, Brandon. 2023. "21 Hand-Picked Knowledge Quotes To Inspire You." *Tettra*. Accessed December 9, 2024. https://tettra.com/article/knowledge-quotes/.

Feldman, Sandra. 2024. "How to Close an LLC: Dissolution, Winding Up, and Termination." *Wolters Kluwer*, July 31. Accessed on December 13, 2024. https://www.wolterskluwer.com/en/expert-insights/dissolving-winding-up-and-terminating-a-limited-liability-company

Field, Anne. 2024. "9 Years After His Shark Tank Splash, Christopher Gray Updates Scholly's Progress." *Forbes*, March 19. Accessed on December 12, 2024. https://www.forbes.com/sites/annefield/2024/03/19/9-years-after-his-shark-tank-splash-christopher-gray-updates-schollys-progress/

Fox, MeiMei. 2021. "3 Entrepreneurs Creating Coffee Alternatives For 2021." *Forbes*, April 29. Accessed on December 12, 2024. https://www.forbes.com/sites/meimeifox/2021/04/28/sick-of-caffeine-jitters-and-afternoon-crashes-here-are-your-2021-coffee-alternatives/

Ghezelbash, Philip. 2024. "Empire Flippers Review: Is It Legit?" *Writing Studio*, January 18. Accessed on December 13, 2024. https://writingstudio.com/blog/empire-flippers-review/

Ghilarducci, Theresa. 2023. "New Study: U.S. Tops Rich Nations As Worst Place To Work." *Forbes*, June 14. Accessed on December 14, 2024. https://www.forbes.com/sites/teresaghilarducci/2023/06/14/new-study-us-tops-rich-nations-in-worst-place-to-work/

Go, Sydney. 2024. "What Are Marketing Automation Tools?" *Semrush*, May 27. Accessed on December 12, 2024. https://www.semrush.com/blog/marketing-automation-tools/

Halton, Clay. 2022. "Inflationary Risk Definition, Ways to Counteract It."

Investopedia, April 19. Accessed on December 12, 2024. https://www.investopedia.com/terms/i/inflationrisk.asp

Hamill, Susan P. 1998. "The Origins Behind the Limited Liability Company." *University of Alabama - Tuscaloosa*. Accessed on December 9, 2024. https://scholarship.law.ua.edu/fac_articles/649/

Harris, Paige. 2022. "5 Reasons Your App Could Be Delisted from Apple's App Store." *Enzuzo*, October 5. Accessed on December 12, 2024. https://www.enzuzo.com/blog/reasons-your-app-could-be-delisted-from-apple-app-store

Hayes, Adam. 2024a. "LLC Operating Agreement: Definition, Purpose, Format, Importance." *Investopedia*, April 22. Accessed on December 10, 2024. https://www.investopedia.com/terms/l/llc-operating-agreement.asp

Hayes, Adam. 2024b. "Franchise Tax: Definition, Rates, Exemptions, and Example." *Investopedia*, May 11. Accessed on December 11, 2024. https://www.investopedia.com/terms/f/franchise_tax.asp

Hayes, Adam. 2024c. "Section 179: Definition, How It Works, and Example." *Investopedia*, January 9. Accessed on December 11, 2024. https://www.investopedia.com/terms/s/section-179.asp

Hayes, Adam. 2024d. "EBITDA: Definition, Calculation Formulas, History, and Criticisms." *Investopedia*, September 6. Accessed on December 13, 2024. https://www.investopedia.com/terms/e/ebitda.asp

Hayes, Adam. 2024e. "Americans With Disabilities Act (ADA): Meaning, History, and Impact." *Investopedia*, January 23. Accessed on December 14, 2024. https://www.investopedia.com/terms/a/americans-with-disabilities-act-ada.asp

Henricks, Mark. 2024. "How to Deduct Health Insurance Premiums If You're Self-Employed." *Smart Asset*, March 5. Accessed on December 11, 2024. https://smartasset.com/insurance/how-to-deduct-health-insurance-premiums-if-youre-self-employed

Herrity, Jennifer. 2024. "What Is Google Analytics? Definition and Benefits." *Indeed*, August 15. Accessed on December 13, 2024. https://www.indeed.com/career-advice/career-development/what-is-google-analytics

Horwitz, Matt. 2023. "LLC Laws by State." *LLC University*, July 1. Accessed on December 14, 2024. https://www.llcuniversity.com/llc-laws-by-state/

Horwitz, Matt. 2024. "How Much Does an LLC Cost by State (2024 Guide)." *LLC University*. Accessed on December 10, 2024. https://www.llcuniversity.com/llc-filing-fees-by-state/

Huston, Heaher. 2021. "LLC vs. Partnership (GP, LP, and LLP): Which Business Structure Is the Best Choice For Multiple Business Owners?" *Wolters Kluwer*, February 3. Accessed on December 9, 2024.

REFERENCES   151

https://www.wolterskluwer.com/en/expert-insights/llc-vs-partnership

Huston, Heather. 2023. "Single-member LLC vs. Sole Proprietorship: Advantages & Disadvantages" *Wolters Kluwer*, November 3. Accessed on December 9, 2024. https://www.wolterskluwer.com/en/expert-insights/singlemember-llc-vs-sole-proprietorship

Internal Revenue Service. 2024a. "Single Member Limited Liability Companies." August 22. Accessed on December 11, 2024. https://www.irs.gov/businesses/small-businesses-self-employed/single-member-limited-liability-companies

Internal Revenue Service. 2024b. "LLC Filing As a Corporation or Partnership." August 22. Accessed on December 11, 2024. https://www.irs.gov/businesses/small-businesses-self-employed/llc-filing-as-a-corporation-or-partnership

Internal Revenue Service. 2024c. "Estimated TRaxes." December 10. Accessed on December 11, 2024. https://www.irs.gov/businesses/small-businesses-self-employed/estimated-taxes

Internal Revenue Service. 2024d. "Small Business Health Care Tax Credit: Questions and Answers." September 13. Accessed on December 12, 2024. https://www.irs.gov/newsroom/small-business-health-care-tax-credit-questions-and-answers

Internal Revenue Service. 2024e. "About Form 1120, U.S. Corporation Income Tax Return." November 12. Accessed on December 14, 2024. https://www.irs.gov/forms-pubs/about-form-1120

Kagan, Julia. 2020. "Income Splitting: What It Means, How It Works." *Investopedia*, November 30. Accessed on December 11, 2024. https://www.investopedia.com/terms/i/incomesplitting.asp

Kagan, Julia. 2024a. "Employer Identification Number (EIN): Who Needs It and How to Get It." *Investopedia*, April 22. Accessed on December 10, 2024. https://www.investopedia.com/terms/e/employer-identification-number.asp

Kagan, Julia. 2024b. "What Is Professional Liability Insurance? Costs and Coverage." *Investopedia*, July 17. Accessed on December 12, 2024. https://www.investopedia.com/terms/p/professional-liability-insurance.asp

Kagan, Julia. 2024c. "Business Interruption Insurance: What It Covers, What It Does Not." *Investopedia*, November 25. Accessed on December 12, 2024. https://www.investopedia.com/terms/b/business-interruption-insurance.asp

Kagan, Julia. 2024d. "What Is a Tax Identification Number (TIN)?" *Investopedia*, March 13. Accessed on December 14, 2024. https://www.investopedia.com/terms/t/tax-indentification-number-tin.asp

Kajtaz, Dzenana. 2023. "What is Email Marketing: In-Depth Guide."

REFERENCES

Mailtrap, February 13. Accessed on December 12, 2024. https://mailtrap.io/blog/email-marketing/

Karamon, Martin, Carolyn Smith Driscoll, and Vivian Kohrs. 2024. "Research & Development (R&D) Tax Credit Frequently Asked Questions." *Cherry Bekaert*, July 11. Accessed on December 11, 2024. https://www.cbh.com/insights/articles/research-development-rd-tax-credit-faqs-answered/

Kenton, Will. 2023. "Fair Labor Standards Act (FLSA) Overview and History." *Investopedia*, December 11. Accessed on December 14, 2024. https://www.investopedia.com/terms/f/fair-labor-standards-act-flsa.asp

Kenton, Will. 2024a. "How to Perform a SWOT Analysis." *Investopedia*, June 29. Accessed on December 10, 2024. https://www.investopedia.com/terms/s/swot.asp

Kenton, Will. 2024b. "Sweat Equity: What It Is, How It Works, and Example." *Investopedia*, July 3. Accessed on December 10, 2024. https://www.investopedia.com/terms/s/sweatequity.asp

Kenton, Will. 2024c. "Business Risk: Definition, Factors, and Examples." *Investopedia*, June 12. Accessed on December 12, 2024. https://www.investopedia.com/terms/b/businessrisk.asp

Kenton, Will. 2024d. "Understanding Liquidity Risk in Banks and Business, With Examples." *Investopedia*, August 22. Accessed on December 12, 2024. https://www.investopedia.com/terms/l/liquidityrisk.asp

Kotlyar, Brian. "What is customer acquisition cost and why does it matter?" *Intercom*. Accessed on December 13, 2024. https://www.intercom.com/blog/what-is-customer-acquisition-cost/

Kurt, Daniel. 2022. "Form 1040-NR: U.S. Nonresident Alien Income Tax Return Explained." *Investopedia*, February 1. Accessed on December 14, 2024. https://www.investopedia.com/form-1040nr-4782170

Langager, Chad. 2024. "Do Non-U.S. Citizens Pay Taxes on Money Earned Through a U.S. Internet Broker?" *Investopedia*, June 18. Accessed on December 14, 2024. https://www.investopedia.com/ask/answers/06/nonusresidenttax.asp

Leslie, Jennifer. 2024. "The Small Business Owner's Guide to Mastering Social Media Advertising." *Keap*, June 27. Accessed on December 12, 2024. https://keap.com/small-business-automation-blog/marketing/social-media/social-media-advertising

Johnson, Heather A. "Trello." *Journal of the Medical Library Association* 105 (2): 209-211. Accessed on December 13, 2024. https://10.5195/jmla.2016.49

Johnson, Holly. 2024. "How to Get a Business Credit Card With an EIN Only." *Bankrate*, September 28. Accessed on December 9, 2024.

REFERENCES

https://www.bankrate.com/credit-cards/business/get-business-card-with-ein/

Maverick, J.B. 2024. "The 5 Licenses and Permits You Need for Your Home-Based Business." *Investopedia*, July 19. Accessed on December 11, 2024. https://www.investopedia.com/articles/personal-finance/120815/licenses-and-permits-you-need-your-homebased-business.asp

McAllister, Neil. 2024. "The Best CRM Software for 2024." *PC Mag*, November 18. Accessed on December 13, 2024. https://www.pcmag.com/picks/the-best-crm-software

Mellgren, Erik. 2023. "US Business Culture: How to Make a Good Impression on American Business Partners." *Globig*, September 13. Accessed on December 14, 2024. https://globig.co/blog/us-business-culture-how-to-make-a-good-impression-on-american-business-partners/

Murphy, Chris B. 2024. "Financial Statements: List of Types and How to Read Them." *Investopedia*, August 4. Accessed on December 12, 2024. https://www.investopedia.com/terms/f/financial-statements.asp

Murphy, Rosalie and Randa Kriss. 2024. "SBA Loan Overview: Types, Pros and Cons, and How to Apply." *NerdWallet*, July 29. Accessed on December 12, 2024. https://www.nerdwallet.com/article/small-business/small-business-loans-sba-loans

National Conference of State Legislatures. 2024. "State Minimum Wages." November 12. Accessed on December 14, 2024. https://www.ncsl.org/labor-and-employment/state-minimum-wages

Nelson, Nikki. 2024. "LLC Electing S Corporation Tax Status: An Option You May Not Know You Have." *Wolters Kluwer*, February 19. Accessed on December 9, 2024. https://www.wolterskluwer.com/en/expert-insights/llc-electing-s-corp-tax-status-an-option-you-may-not-know-you-have

Nevins, Mark. 2023. "How To Get Stuff Done: The Eisenhower Matrix (a.k.a. The Urgent Vs The Important)." *Forbes*, January 5. Accessed on December 13, 2024. https://www.forbes.com/sites/hillennevins/2023/01/05/how-to-get-stuff-done-the-eisenhower-matrix-aka-the-urgent-vs-the-important/

O'Neill, Aaron. 2024. "Twenty Countries With the Largest Population in 2024." *Statista*, July 4. Accessed on December 14, 2024. https://www.statista.com/statistics/262879/countries-with-the-largest-population/

Odegard, Jenny. 2018. "What's The Deal With New York's LLC Publication Requirement?" *Forbes*, April 5. Accessed on December 11, 2024. https://www.forbes.com/sites/jennyodegard/2017/09/06/whats-the-deal-with-new-yorks-llc-publication-requirement/

Orem, Tina. 2024. "Home Office Tax Deduction 2024: Rules, Who Qualifies." *NerdWallet*, October 9. Accessed on December 11, 2024. https://www.nerdwallet.com/article/taxes/home-office-tax-deduction

Payne, Ronald D. "What Happens If You Miss the LLC Annual Report Deadline?" *Apple Payne Law*. Accessed on December 11, 2024. https://applepaynelaw.com/blog/llc-annual-report-deadline/

Porter, T.J. "LLC Mistakes That Put Your Liability at Risk." *Collective*. Accessed on December 11, 2024. https://www.collective.com/blog/llc-mistakes-risk-liability

Prakash, Priyanka. 2020. "Member-Managed LLC vs. Manager-Managed LLC: Which Should You Choose?" *NerdWallet*, October 14. Accessed on December 9, 2024. https://www.nerdwallet.com/article/small-business/member-managed-llc

Prakash, Priyanka. 2024. "LLC Operating Agreement: Benefits and How to Write One." *NerdWallet*, September 20. Accessed on December 10, 2024. https://www.nerdwallet.com/article/small-business/llc-operating-agreement

Rich, Stanley R. and David E. Gumpert. 1985. "How to Write a Winning Business Plan." *Harvard Business Review*. Accessed on December 10, 2024. https://hbr.org/1985/05/how-to-write-a-winning-business-plan

Schmidt, Laura. 2024. "Doing Business in Another State (Foreign Qualification)." *Wolters Kluwer*, January 12. Accessed on December 14, 2024. https://www.wolterskluwer.com/en/expert-insights/doing-business-in-another-state-foreign-qualification

Segal, Troy. 2024. "Estate Planning: 16 Things to Do Before You Die." *Investopedia*, May 19. Accessed on December 13, 2024. https://www.investopedia.com/articles/retirement/10/estate-planning-checklist.asp

Simons, Tad. 2024. "How Are LLCs Taxed? LLC Tax Benefits and Tips to Reduce Taxes." *Thomson Reuters*, February 8. Accessed on December 11, 2024. https://tax.thomsonreuters.com/blog/how-are-llcs-taxed-llc-tax-benefits-and-tips-to-reduce-taxes/

SimplifyLLC. 2024. "How Long Does it Take Form an LLC and Get Approved?" August 9. Accessed on December 10, 2024. https://www.simplifyllc.com/llc-glossary/how-long-does-it-take-to-get-an-llc/

Steingold, David M. 2024. "LLC Articles of Organization." *Nolo*, July 19. Accessed on December 10, 2024. https://www.nolo.com/legal-encyclopedia/llc-articles-organization.html

Team Jobvite. 2024. "The Real Cost of Employee Turnover (And How to Prevent It)." *Jobvite*, August 14. Accessed on December 12, 2024. https://www.jobvite.com/blog/cost-of-employee-turnover/

The Investopedia Team. 2024. "Credit Risk: Definition, Role of Ratings, and Examples." *Investopedia*, September 23. Accessed on December 12, 2024. https://www.investopedia.com/terms/c/creditrisk.asp

REFERENCES 155

The Scholarship System. 2024. "What is the Scholly Scholarships App & Does it Work?" April 14. Accessed on December 12, 2024. https://thescholarshipsystem.com/blog-for-students-families/what-is-the-scholly-scholarships-app-does-it-work/

Thomson Reuters. 2024. "Pass-Through Entity." February 14. Accessed on December 9, 2024. https://tax.thomsonreuters.com/en/glossary/pass-through-entity

Thomson Reuters Tax & Accounting. 2024. "Understanding Form 1042-S." *Thomson Reuters*, March 5. Accessed on December 14, 2024. https://tax.thomsonreuters.com/blog/understanding-form-1042-s/

Tuovila, Alicia. 2024. "Capital Account Explained: How It Works and Why It's Important." *Investopedia*, September 3. Accessed on December 10, 2024. https://www.investopedia.com/terms/c/capitalaccount.asp

Twin, Alexandra. 2024. "Property Insurance: Definition and How Coverage Works." *Investopedia*, July 18. Accessed on December 12, 2024. https://www.investopedia.com/terms/p/property-insurance.asp

Tyler, Brad. 2024. "What is a Limited Liability Company (LLC)?" *Bank of America*, July 10. Accessed on December 9, 2024. https://business.bankofamerica.com/resources/what-is-a-limited-liability-company-llc.html

Upcounsel. 2020. "Well Known LLC Companies: Everything You Need to Know," July 8. Accessed on December 10, 2024. https://www.upcounsel.com/well-known-llc-companies

U.S. Citizenship and Immigration Services. 2024. "International Entrepreneur Rule." October 11. Accessed on December 14, 2024. https://www.uscis.gov/working-in-the-united-states/international-entrepreneur-rule

U.S. Department of the Treasury. 2024. "U.S. Beneficial Ownership Information Registry Now Accepting Reports." January 1. Accessed on December 11, 2024. https://home.treasury.gov/news/press-releases/jy2015

Vanian, Jonathan and Dan Mangan. 2024. "Appeals Court Upholds Law Ordering China-Based ByteDance to Sell TikTok or Face U.S. Ban." *CNBC*, December 6. Accessed on December 12, 2024. https://www.cnbc.com/2024/12/06/tiktok-divestment-law-upheld-by-federal-appeals-court.html

Vethan Law Firm, P.C. 2017. "LLC Member Withdrawal: How to Get Out of Your Limited Liability Company." May 23. Accessed on December 9, 2024. https://vethanlaw.com/blog/2017/05/llc-member-withdrawal-how-to-get-out-of-your-limited-liability-company/

Wallace, Mike. 2024. "IRS Form 5472: Filing Requirements and Tips." *Greenback Expat Tax Services*, October 10. Accessed on December 14,

REFERENCES

2024. https://www.greenbacktaxservices.com/knowledge-center/form-5472/

White, Jeremy. 2020. "The Secrets Behind the Runaway Success of Apple's AirPods." *Wired*, May 9. Accessed on December 12, 2024. https://www.wired.com/story/apple-airpods-success/

Willis, Andrea A. 2023. "Can an LLC Own Another LLC?" *Lawyer for Business*, June 5. Accessed on December 9, 2024. https://lawyerforbusiness.com/blog/can-an-llc-own-another-llc

Wong, Belle. 2024a. "How to Add Capital Contributions to an LLC." *Legal Zoom*, March 21. Accessed on December 10, 2024. https://www.legalzoom.com/articles/how-to-add-capital-contributions-to-an-llc

Wong, Belle. 2024b. "What Is a Registered Agent? A Business Compliance Guide." *Legal Zoom*, July 18. Accessed on December 10, 2024. https://www.legalzoom.com/articles/what-is-a-registered-agent

Woodside, Jennifer. 2024a. "How Are Profits Split in an LLC?" *Wolters Kluwer*, January 12. Accessed on December 9, 2024. https://www.wolterskluwer.com/en/expert-insights/how-are-profits-split-in-an-llc

Woodside, Jennifer. 2024b. "LLC Pass-Through Taxation: What Small Business Owners Need to Know." *Wolters Kluwer*, September 16. Accessed on December 11, 2024. https://www.wolterskluwer.com/en/expert-insights/llc-pass-through-taxation-what-small-business-owners-need-to-know

Yakal, Kathy. 2024a. "Zoho Books Review." *PC Mag*, October 23. Accessed on December 11, 2024. https://www.pcmag.com/reviews/zoho-books

Yakal, Kathy. 2024b. "Intuit QuickBooks Online Review." *PC Mag*, October 21. Accessed on December 11, 2024. https://www.pcmag.com/reviews/intuit-quickbooks-online

Yasar, Kinza. 2024. "What is Search Engine Optimization (SEO)?" *TechTarget*, October. Accessed on December 12, 2024. https://www.techtarget.com/whatis/definition/search-engine-optimization-SEO

Zitron, Ed. 2024. "Bubble Trouble." *Where's Your Ed*, April 4. Accessed on December 12, 2024. https://www.wheresyoured.at/bubble-trouble/

Made in the USA
Monee, IL
13 June 2025